CONTENTS

Introduction

After making quilts for twenty-five years, I look back and I am amazed at how much quilting techniques have changed. Women have always been interested in experimenting with quilting and many wonderful designs and developments have come about as a result.

When I first began quilting, I made templates, marked around them on single layers of fabric, and hand pieced the seams. When I finally owned a sewing machine, I worked with techniques that would allow me to make different templates, mark around them and cut multiple layers of fabric at one time, and sew the seams on the sewing machine.

Despite the success with these techniques, I was always frustrated at these slow and often inaccurate methods. The minute you start marking around a template, the line varies from the actual desired shape.

When the rotary cutter came out, it was an immediate success. People who were using the strip piecing techniques, such as Seminole and strip garments, went crazy. At last, the measurements you desired could be cut with no marking at all. Many quilt makers were dreaming up faster and faster methods of achieving quilts with little hassle. Template-free sewing is everywhere. The rotary cutter took us well beyond the strips. Many other shapes are possible and we shall explore them.

The intention of this book is not to bring you techniques that are altogether new, but to organize known techniques into a format that will help you think differently about sewing quilts. The first section of this book will give you the basic skills needed for piecing quilts. The second section will give you eight quilt patterns that use these techniques. Cutting guides and directions are provided to make nineteen various sized quilts. These quilts are not only fast, but above all they are accurate.

I have always been interested in the math of quiltmaking; therefore, I will attempt to explain the math involved in planning and executing these quilts. Don't worry, there are only four formulas that you will be using. Understanding these formulas will enable you to plan your own quilts.

"Accuracy counts" is a saying in many fields. It is just as true in quilt-making. No one likes to apologize for a pieced quilt that is filled with intersections that do not meet, points of triangles that are cut off, and quilts that will not lie flat. The techniques covered in this book will help guide you to mathematically correct and well-sewn quilts of which you can be proud.

For those of you who prefer hand piecing, these cutting techniques will work for you as well. Independent pieces can be cut without marking around templates. With accurately cut shapes, all you need to do is draw a seam line inside the cut lines and proceed with your hand piecing. Cutting multiple layers accurately will save you much time.

Tools and Rules

Equipment

The secret to this system of quiltmaking is the equipment you will use. With the right equipment and techniques, quiltmaking can be accurate as well as fast.

The first thing you will need will be a rotary cutter. It comes in two sizes, but I recommend the larger heavy-duty one which is much easier to use. You will have better control. When the cutters first came out they did not have a good cutting surface, and I almost gave up on them. Olfa™ came out with its mat, however, and it made all the difference in the world. First, the matte finish helps hold the fabric in place and it is easy to cut on. Second, it protects the blade and the table you are cutting on. A mat that will allow you to cut the fabric as it comes off the bolt will be the best size (approximately 18″ x 24″).

You will also need a tool both to measure and to guide your cutter, ensuring a clean straight cut. The Rotary Rule™ is a cutting tool designed for use in template-free quiltmaking. It is made of ¼″ thick Plexiglas™. Anything thinner would not stabilize the cutter and would most likely get cut up. The Rotary Rule™ has a ruler down its length and is graduated in ¼″ increments across the width so that you can measure right to left. To do more advanced procedures, it is very handy to have 45° angle markings and even nicer to have a 60° angle printed on it. It has three perpendicular intersecting lines across the width to help you subcut strips with straight square cuts. When we come to learning about triangles, the ruler is used to measure these as well. On the Rotary Rule™, there are dotted lines on some of the ⅛″ lines. These lines make short work of cutting accurate triangles. There are other Plexiglas™ rulers on the market. If you are using one of these, make sure it has these features.

In addition to the Rotary Rule™, I have found a Mini-Quilters Rule™ very handy. These are six-inch Plexiglas™ squares that are easy to handle when short cuts are needed and also will enable you to extend your ruler up to nine inches or nine and one-half inches when wider cuts are called for.

In addition to these tools, I find a right triangle very helpful. One that is 12″ on a side is the most useful. I like my fluorescent-colored one, because when my sewing room looks like a rummage sale, I can find it among the unsorted piles.

It is so important to work with the best tools possible. "The right tool for the right job" is really true. Shortcutting some of the boring procedures in quilting gets you to the enjoyable parts faster.

Slice and Dice

It is very important to learn to use the rotary equipment accurately and efficiently. Since we want to work with straight pieces, we must work with perfectly straight cut strips.

The first thing is to straighten the fabric. We will be working with "close grain" as it is almost impossible to straighten fabric these days, since the threads are often far from perpendicular. You will need to make clean cuts rather than cuts that are exactly on the straight of the grain.

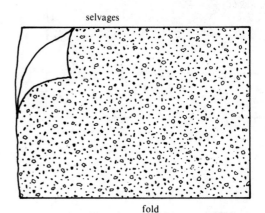

selvages

fold

1. Fold the fabric in half, selvage to selvage, the way it comes off the bolt.

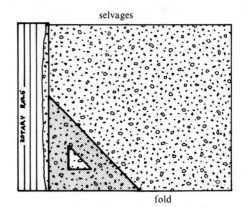

selvages

fold

2. Lay the triangle along the folded edge of the fabric and push against the right side of the ruler until you are just at the edge. (If you are right-handed, the bulk of the fabric should be coming from the right.)

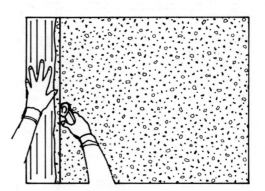

3. Hold the ruler down with your left hand and begin cutting slightly in front of the fold, walk your hand up parallel with the cutter and continue to cut right off the end of the fabric. If you try to hold onto the ruler at the bottom and cut to the end of it, you most likely will move it and therefore cut inaccurately. This is the only time you will have to cut such a long slice.

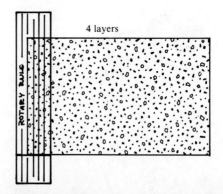

4 layers

4. Then, fold the fabric one more time, lining up the cut edges. Using markings on the ruler, cut the appropriate strip width. Now cuts can be made only 11″ long. This is much easier. I try to check about every 18″ along the length of the fabric to see if I am still straight. I do this by opening up the fabric, using the triangle and ruler again just to check if I am still perpendicular to the first fold.

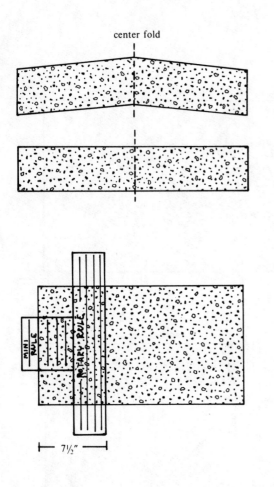

center fold

If cuts are not perpendicular to the fold, strips will have V shapes in them when you open them up to sew. Everything is cut selvage to selvage, so you will become aware of this soon enough.

When you need to cut the fabric wider than 3½″ you can combine the width of the ruler with any portion of the 6″ Mini-Rule. You will find most of the cuts in the book will be 3½″ or less. If you have cuts wider than the two rulers combined, use the side of the longer ruler to measure off the desired width.

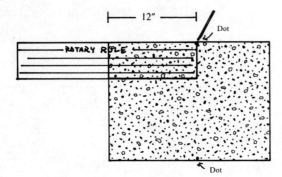

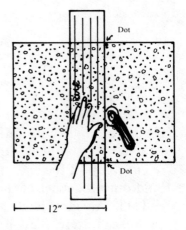

8

Subcutting into Squares and Rectangles

Some designs will require independent squares or rectangles. These "loose" units will be cut from strips.

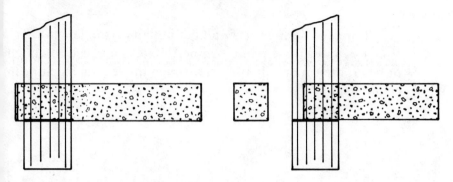

1. Cut strips the width of the unit plus seam allowances. Then, working with at least four layers at a time, straighten the left edge of the strips (usually has the selvages and maybe a fold) by placing the cut edge on the halfway line of the ruler and making a perpendicular slice.

2. Then, measure left to right, cutting squares the same width as the strips.

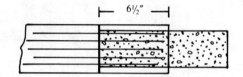
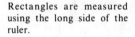

Rectangles are measured using the long side of the ruler.

Subcutting Sewn Strips

Many designs begin merely as cut strips. These strips are sewn together, pressed and then cut again. Four Patches and Nine Patches are best pieced this way and these units occur over and over in other pieced blocks.

In a Four Patch, sew together two sets of contrasting strips.

4 Patch   9 Patch

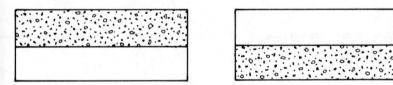

Press consistently toward the same color.

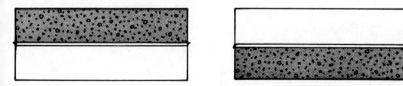

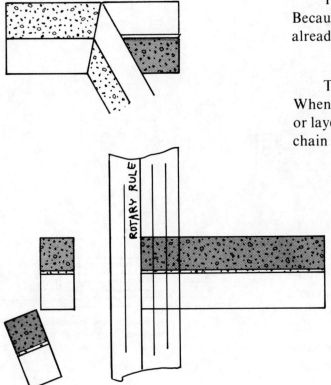

Then place these two sewn strips right sides together. Because of your pressing you will find the seam allowances already going in the opposite directions.

Trim the selvages off and cut in pairs from left to right. When you sew these pairs together, there is no need to match or layer; they are ready to feed through the sewing machine in chain fashion.

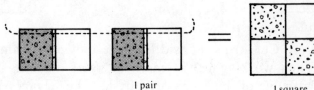

1 pair = 1 square

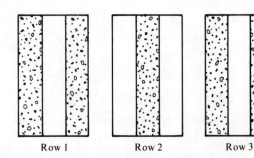

Row 1   Row 2   Row 3

In a Nine Patch the same technique applies, only this time you have three sets of three sewn strips.

Place rows one and two together. Cut into pairs and sew together in chain fashion.

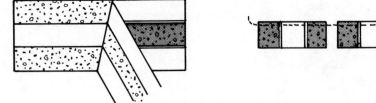

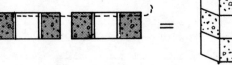

Row three is cut by itself.
These strips are then added, to end up with the three rows sewn together.

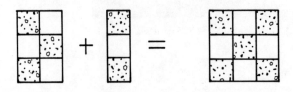

Sewing Guidelines

The other invaluable tool is obviously the sewing machine. Many of you are quite adept at the sewing machine already and may or may not have had success at piecing quilts. The sewing machine has been given a bad name in quiltmaking, yet it has been used in making quilts for the past 125 years. There are quilts dated the same year as its introduction.

Along with cutting accurately, sewing accurately will yield pieced quilt tops of which you can be proud. No one enjoys sewing and resewing to make things come out correctly. Here are a few guidelines to help you keep on track. Usually, when I see work that looks sloppy or haphazardly pieced, one of these rules was broken.

SINCE ¼″ SEAM ALLOWANCES ARE ADDED TO ALL CUT PIECES, YOU MUST LEARN TO SEW ¼″ SEAMS. No matter what type of sewing machine you are working on, you will have to establish where to look ON THE PRESSER FOOT as a guide to yield the correct seam. Very few machines have a presser foot exactly ¼″ wide. If you are lucky enough to have one, be happy, as most of us do not.

The reason I say ON THE PRESSER FOOT is because for some of the techniques in this book, you will not be able to see the bed of the machine. Therefore, any markings on the bed, such as masking tape or the machine's own markings, will not help you later. That method works if you are always sewing independent pieces, but it is limiting.

All you have to do is take a piece of fabric and feed it through your machine at what you feel is ¼″ away from the needle. THEN MEASURE IT.

I have a foreign-made machine and the ¼″ seam means I must keep the edge of the fabric just under the presser foot. When you practice enough, it really becomes easy. People who do a great deal of piecing become so familiar with what a ¼″ seam looks like that they can spot anything that deviates from it. When sewing long strips it is natural to drift, but if you try to remember the trouble it causes, you will stay steady.

WHEN SEWING TWO PIECES TOGETHER THAT ARE SUPPOSED TO MATCH, IT IS UP TO YOU TO MAKE SURE THEY BEGIN AND END MATCHED. All machines have a tendency to shift layers of fabric. If you think of your machine as an opponent that is purposely trying to shift everything, you hold on and make sure that it can't. I do not pin, but if you feel it will ensure that the pieces match, then by all means pin.

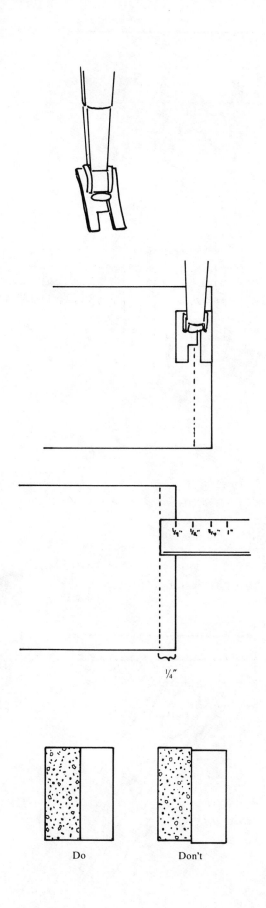

¼″

Do   Don't

11

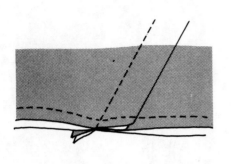

WHEN COMING TO INTERSECTING SEAMS, SEAM ALLOWANCES SHOULD ALWAYS GO OPPOSITE DIRECTIONS. Your machine really wants to jog any bulky areas. If you line up all seams going the same way, it will most likely move one. By having seams going opposite directions, the bulk is reduced and this helps the seams hug that intersection. You want this intersection to look crisp from the front.

It is not unusual in machine piecing to have seams twist and change directions in order to make seam allowances go in opposite directions.

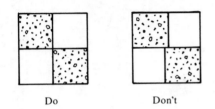

Do   Don't

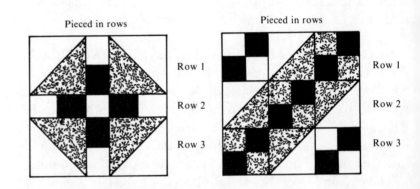

In most machine-pieced designs, blocks are pieced in rows or in quarters. If you take a minute to decide which way would be best for the particular block you are working on, you can be more efficient in your piecing.

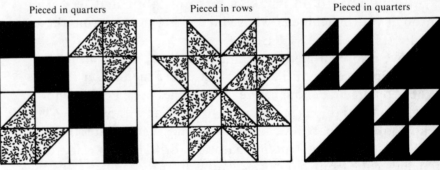

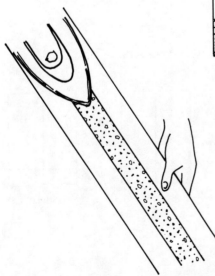

As a rule, seams are not pressed open in machine piecing. They are pressed to one side, usually toward the darker fabric. When pressing sets of strips, you will find it better to press from the right side. That way they are pressed completely flat, and you are less likely to press pleats at the seams. On many patterns, the direction of the pressing is the key to ensuring a neat and correctly pieced quilt.

12

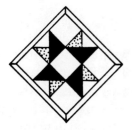

Triangles

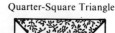
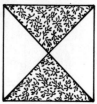

Quarter-Square Triangle

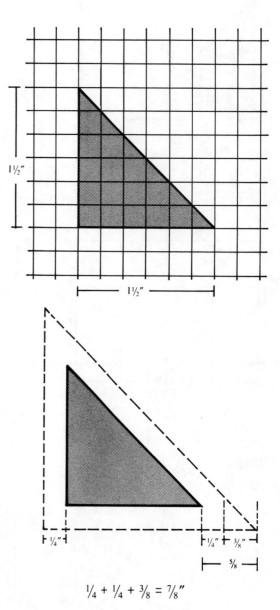

Half-Square Triangle

We tend to think of using the rotary cutter only for quilts made of strips. This is very limiting. Other shapes can be cut with the rotary cutter as well.

Once you start adding triangles to squares and rectangles, hundreds of patterns are possible. The techniques in this book are fast, easy, and accurate.

First of all, I will be talking about two different triangles. One I will refer to as a half-square triangle and the other as a quarter-square triangle.

Half-Square Triangles

A half-square triangle is half of a square and is measured on the two shorter sides. These sides are on grain.

When a square is subdivided into four triangles, they are referred to as quarter-square triangles. A quarter-square triangle is a right triangle that has the long side on grain. It is with this measurement that we will be concerned. We need to make this distinction in the use of these triangles because the outside edge of every square and the outside edge of every quilt is easier to handle if on grain.

If you were to draft a triangle on a piece of graph paper and add a $\frac{1}{4}''$ seam allowance all around, you would find an interesting phenomenon. The difference between the finished edges of the triangle and the cut edges with the seam allowance is not what you would expect. The straight side has $\frac{1}{4}''$ difference, yet the pointed side has $\frac{5}{8}''$ difference between the finished and the cut point. We expected $\frac{1}{4}''$, yet there is an additional $\frac{3}{8}''$. Therefore, for us to use triangles, we must remember this fact: **The formula for half-square triangles is the finished size plus $\frac{7}{8}''$.**

$$\frac{1}{4} + \frac{1}{4} + \frac{3}{8} = \frac{7}{8}''$$

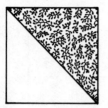

Half Square Triangles

Fast Sewn Half-Square Triangles

Fast triangles are not new. Many have written about them; you can hardly pick up a pattern anymore without running into instructions using this technique. However, some of these instructions tell you to add one inch to the measurement of the triangle. So, adding one inch is a $\frac{1}{8}''$ miscalculation. Multiplied over many pieces, this can add up to one big headache. Things suddenly don't fit and it can be very discouraging.

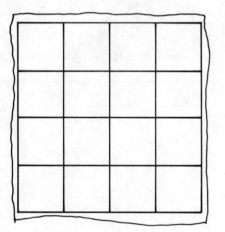

Establish 2 perpendicular lines with your triangle. Draw these lines on the lightest fabric.

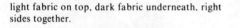

light fabric on top, dark fabric underneath, right sides together.

When you are making patterns where two different color triangles are sewn together to form a square, you will sew them first. Working with 2 fat quarters of fabric (each 18″ by 22″) placed right sides together, you will mark a grid of squares with the formula; the finished size of the triangle plus $\frac{7}{8}''$. For every square you draw, you will get two sewn triangle units.

Draw the diagonals through all squares, first in one direction marking every other row of squares, then marking the alternate squares with a diagonal in the opposite direction.

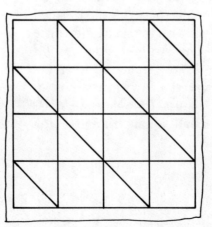 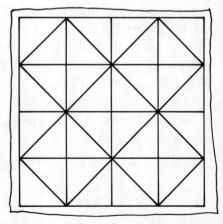

If you have established where ¼″ is on your presser foot, you can use that as a guide and stitch a ¼″ seam on both sides of all the diagonals. Because of the way you have drawn the diagonals, you will find you can just keep stitching without stopping. It reminds me of when I learned to draw a house with one continuous line in the third grade. This triangle method is still as exciting to me now as drawing the house was then.

If you have trouble with the proper seam allowance, you could use your ruler and mark ¼″ lines on each side of the diagonals and just stitch on the lines. It will be slower, but more accurate.

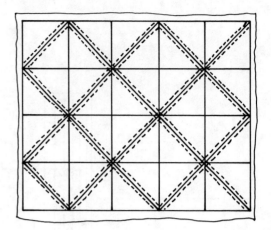

After these are sewn, cut them apart exactly on the drawn lines. I found that if you cut them into squares first, you can clip out the points before you subcut them into triangles. These points are not in the way when pressing or sewing into the design. The resulting square made up of these two triangles will measure correctly.

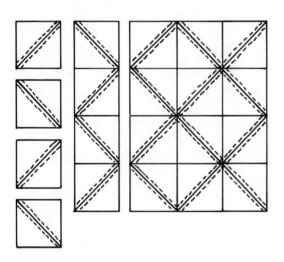

Clip out points

1 square

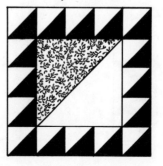

Goose in the Pond   Lady of the Lake

Loose Half-Square Triangles

If you are dealing with patterns where these triangles used separately, the formula still holds.

Cut a strip the desired finished measurement plus ⁷⁄₈″.

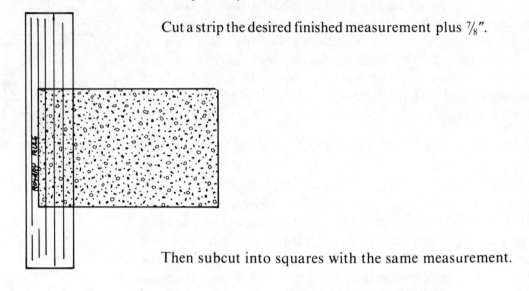

Then subcut into squares with the same measurement.

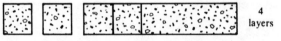

Take a stack of four squares and cut diagonally corner to corner once. These triangles are now the right size to mix with the other shapes.

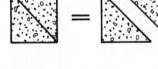

Northumberland Star

Farmer's Daughter

16

Quarter-Square Triangles

Quarter-square triangles are important, as they form the sides of an Ohio Star, the bottom of Flying Geese, and turn up over and over in blocks and borders. The long side of this triangle needs to be on grain to keep the block or border from being stretchy. The long side is the measurement that you usually know.

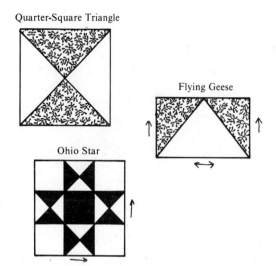

Quarter-Square Triangle

Flying Geese

Ohio Star

Sewn Quarter-Square Triangles

If you draw a quarter-square triangle on graph paper, putting the long side on grain and drawing the seam allowance, you will find two points with $5/8''$ sticking out from the finished points. The sum of these is $1\frac{1}{4}''$. **So the formula for dealing with a quarter-square triangle is the finished measurement of the long side plus $1\frac{1}{4}''$.**

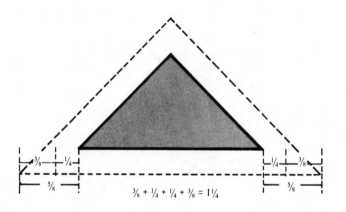

$\frac{3}{8} + \frac{1}{4} + \frac{1}{4} + \frac{3}{8} = 1\frac{1}{4}$

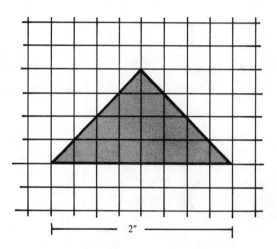

2"

Sometimes, quarter-square triangles are to be sewn first. The formula is still the same, but first you will draw the squares, mark with an X, then stitch.

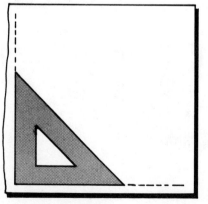

light fabric on top, dark fabric underneath, right sides together.

Establish 2 perpendicular lines with your triangle.

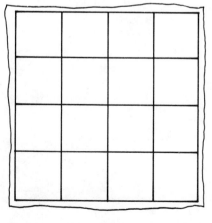

Draw a grid, the finished size of the triangle's long edge plus $1\frac{1}{4}''$.

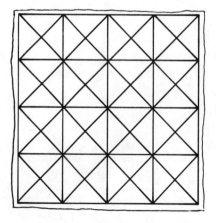

Draw an X through all squares.

17

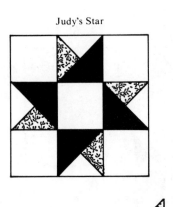

Judy's Star

How you stitch these two fabrics is decided by the design you are making. As in Judy's Star, one of the triangles is consistently on the same side of the other triangle. To deal with this the stitching may seem strange.

You will sew on alternate sides of the drawn lines. Each time you start down a diagonal line, begin with the same side. For instance, always start with the right side of the diagonal. When you get to the cross lines, switch your stitching to the other side. Continue this way down the diagonal. When stitching is done down all the diagonals, cut on all drawn lines. The result will be triangles in the same order, long sides on grain.

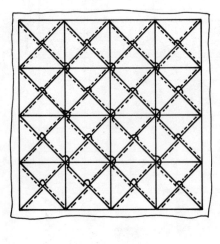

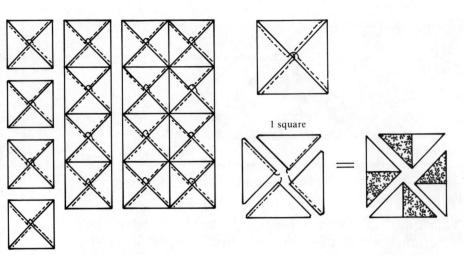

1 square

In designs where this unit is used along with its mirror image, the grid is made the same but the stitching is different. Stitch down both sides of the diagonals going in one direction only.

Castle in the Air

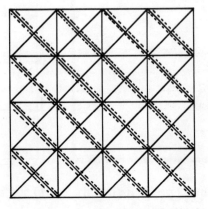

Mirror Images

18

Loose Quarter-Square Triangles

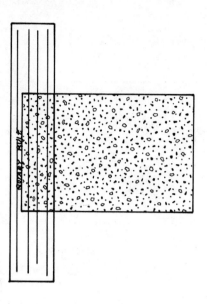

If these are cut and used independently:
Cut a strip the desired finished measurement plus 1¼″.

Then subcut into squares with the same measurement.

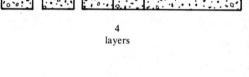

4
layers

Then with a stack of these squares (at least four) cut an X by lining up the ruler from corner to opposite corner. Without moving these pieces, cut in the other direction. Each square will yield four triangles with the long side on grain.

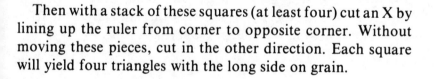
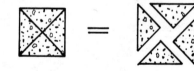

NOTE: When these are used in quilts in the pattern section, I will refer to the sewn quarter-square triangles as a square **sewn** with an X. If these quarter-square triangles are to be used loose, then I will tell you to cut a square with an X.

Mini-Triangles

When a design calls for half-square triangles smaller than 1½″, making triangles with the fast triangle method can be difficult. The marking and sewing are easy; it is the pressing that presents the problem. The triangle squares are so small it is easy to distort them, not to mention burning your fingers.

An alternate method of making fast triangles is the bias strip method. This method is covered by Marsha McCloskey in *Projects for Blocks and Borders*. We must adapt this to the rotary cutter, which speeds up the technique.

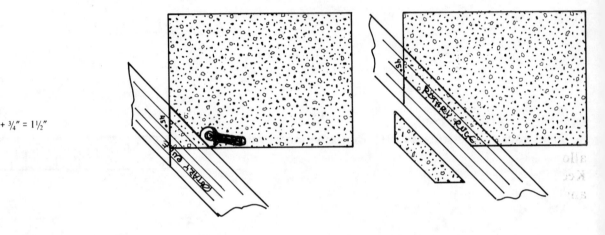

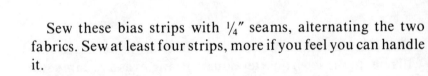

¾″

+ ¾″ = 1½″

Figure the size triangle you are trying to make. Add ¾ - 1″ to the finished size and cut bias strips this measurement from each fabric used in the triangle squares.

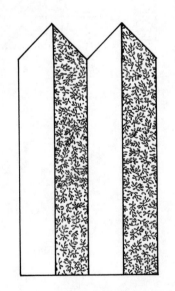

Sew these bias strips with ¼″ seams, alternating the two fabrics. Sew at least four strips, more if you feel you can handle it.

Line up the 45° angle in the center of the ruler with one of the seams and cut.

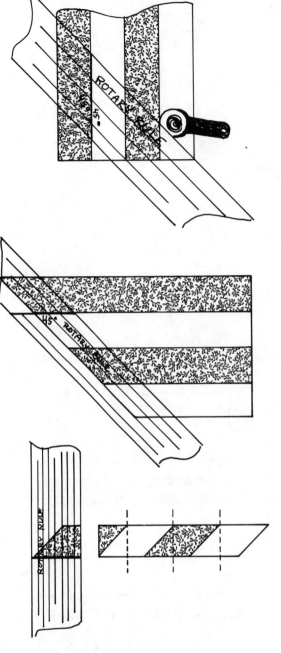

Then line up the desired square size (plus the ½" seam allowance) on the ruler and make strips that measurement. Keep the 45° angle line on a stitching line to stay at the correct angle.

Lining up the straight cut edge with the straight line on the ruler, cut perpendicularly where the point ends on the edge.

Turn pieces around and cut finished measurement plus ½".

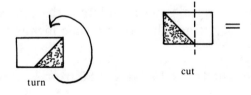

There is very little waste. This technique will work best for very small triangles. There is a lot of interest in miniature quilts, and one of the stumbling blocks is ironing these small units and avoiding distorting them.

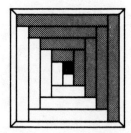

Precision Log Cabins

The template-free method is ideal for making Log Cabin quilts, since this quilt is made from strips. The entire quilt can be pre-cut before you begin sewing. Each "log" will be cut a specific length, by measuring along the length of your ruler, reading from right to left.

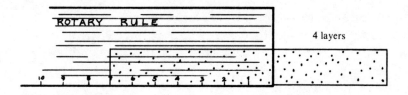

You will be able to cut 6 to 8 layers at a time, then organize the stacks of strips at your sewing area in assembly line fashion.

A common problem with Log Cabin blocks is they often are not the same size when finished. Pre-cut the "logs" to a specific length, ensuring accuracy when each strip is sewn. Therefore, all blocks are square and the same size after piecing.

Special Tip:

If selecting fabrics is your stumbling block, choose one light fabric and repeat it on the light side of the quilt. This will simplify the number of fabrics you will need to select and give a more dramatic look to your quilt design.

If strips are cut 1½" wide you will need the following amounts of fabric to make a quilt 72" by 90" set 8 blocks by 10 blocks without borders:

In cutting strips to length, you will end up with a stack of 80 units for each log. (Cutting 8 layers at a time means only 10 cuts)

Center squares are cut 1½" x 1½" — cut 80 from ¼ yard.

Light fabric (4¾ yards) Make cuts 1½", 2½", 3½", 4½", 5½", 6½", 7½" and 8½". Cut the longest logs first, then the shorter lengths from leftover strips.

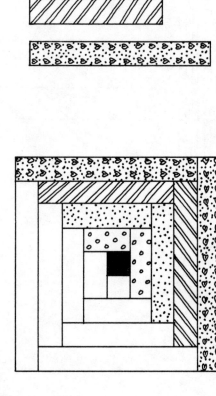

First Dark — (¾ yd.) cut 2½" and 3½" lengths.
Second Dark — (1 yd.) cut 4½" and 5½" lengths.
Third Dark — (1½ yd.) cut 6½" and 7½" lengths.
Fourth Dark — (1¾ yd.) cut 8½" and 9½" lengths.

Diagonally Set Quilts

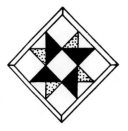

Diagonally set quilts are wonderful to behold. A block that you are familiar with set straight will often look altogether different when set on point. Many people steer away from them because they seem too hard to plan.

In planning a diagonally set quilt there are a few things you have to take into consideration. First, in order to figure how many blocks you will need, you need to know the diagonal measurement of the block.

It is very simple to figure. You will know the finished measurement of the block. Simply multiply that number by 1.414 and that will yield the diagonal measurement. It is the diagonal measurement that determines the finished size of the quilt.

This chart will save you the time of figuring your own diagonals.

SIZE OF BLOCK	DIAGONAL	SIZE OF BLOCK	DIAGONAL
2	2.83	11.5	16.26
2.5	3.54	12	16.97
3	4.24	12.5	17.68
3.5	4.95	13	18.38
4	5.66	13.5	19.09
4.5	6.36	14	19.80
5	7.07	14.5	20.50
5.5	7.78	15	21.21
6	8.48	15.5	21.92
6.5	9.19	16	22.62
7	9.90	16.5	23.33
7.5	10.61	17	24.04
8	11.31	17.5	24.75
8.5	12.02	18	25.45
9	12.73	18.5	26.16
9.5	13.43	19	26.87
10	14.14	19.5	27.57
10.5	14.85	20	28.28
11	15.55	20.5	28.99

Two Types of Diagonally Set Quilts

There are two types of diagonally set quilts. To determine which is which, tilt your head sideways and look at the first row.

One type of diagonally set quilt starts off with one block in the first diagonal row. In each row after that the number of blocks increases by two. All rows contain an odd number of blocks. To figure the finished size of the quilt, you can count how many diagonals across and down you will have. Multiply this by the diagonal measurement of the block.

If you want a rectangular quilt instead of a square one, you count the number of blocks in the row that establishes the width and repeat that number in following rows until the desired length is established.

Square Quilt

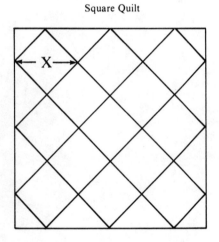

Rectangular Quilt

This row establishes quilt width

repeat for desired length

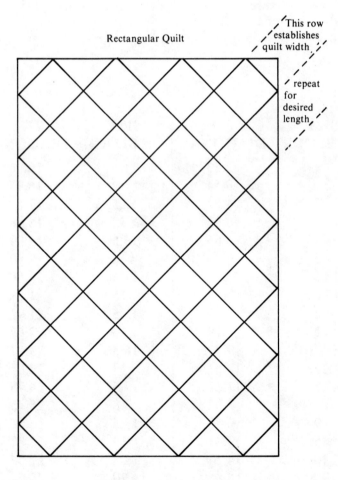

The second type of diagonally set quilt has two blocks in the first diagonal row. This quilt usually has even numbers of blocks in the rows. It is important to remember that the second row establishes the width and length of the quilt.

When lengthening these quilts, something unusual happens. You will go from an even number to an odd number of blocks in a row, then back to even numbers.

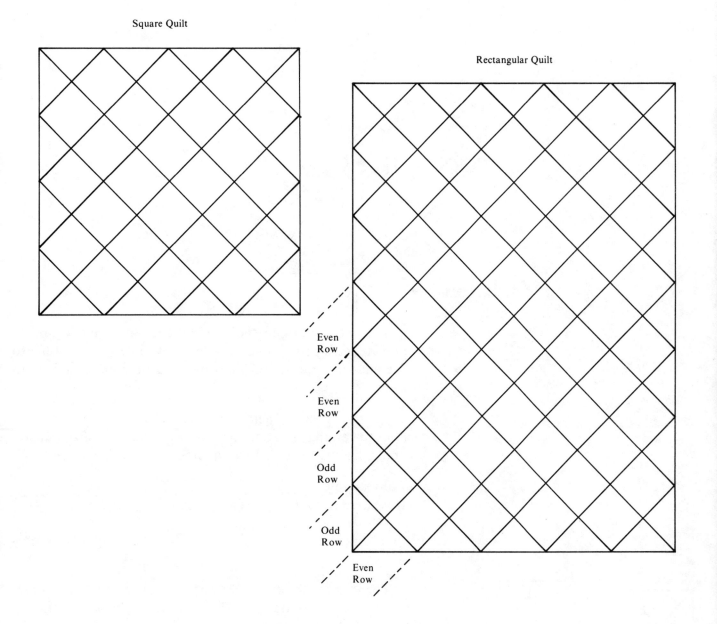

Square Quilt

Rectangular Quilt

Even Row

Even Row

Odd Row

Odd Row

Even Row

Setting Triangles

All diagonally set quilts are pieced in rows starting in a corner, each row containing a setting triangle at each end. Here you have a quarter-square triangle that forms the outside of the quilt.

Setting Triangles

You must first figure the diagonal measurement of the block you are setting (diagonal equals the side times 1.414). Refer to the chart on page 23. This is the measurement you need to know.

To this measurement, you can add the $1\frac{1}{4}''$ for seam allowances and the resulting number is the size of the square you will have to cut. These squares are cut off of strips.

For example:
If you are to set 6″ squares .... $6 \times 1.414 = 8\frac{1}{2}$

$$8\frac{1}{2} + 1\frac{1}{4} = 9\frac{3}{4}$$

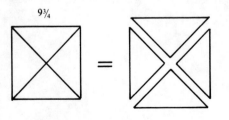

Then subcut these squares with an X. Each of these squares yields 4 setting triangles. These triangles will then fit the finished blocks exactly.

26

If you want these squares to float inside the border or binding, you can make these setting triangles larger than you need. You will still have to know the diagonal measurement of the block, but you double the seam allowance that is added to the diagonal measurement. So instead of 1¼″ added to the long measurement, add 2½″.

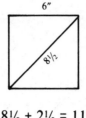

$8\frac{1}{2} + 2\frac{1}{2} = 11$

Non-floating

Floating

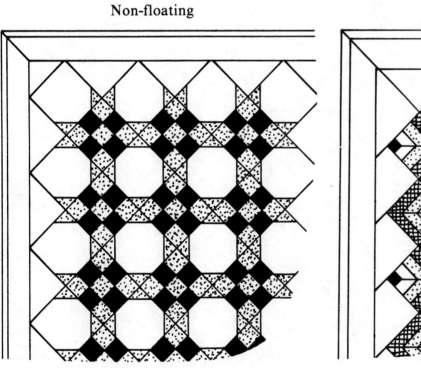 

27

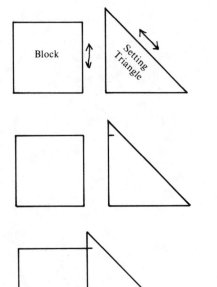

Now comes a tip on fitting triangles to the block and still remaining accurate on the outside of the quilt.

When these larger squares are cut into an X, the resulting triangles will be too large; there is also the additional challenge of having the sides being bias.

It is easy to handle these if you will mark the side of the triangle with a slight notch to show where the block will fit, and make sure only this portion of the triangle is sewn onto the block.

The seam will intersect at ¼" from the edge.

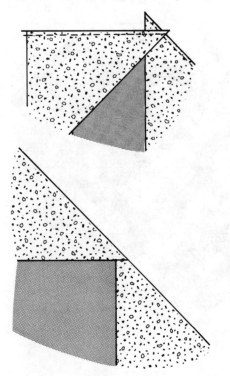

When joining rows, make sure the seams of the last intersecting blocks are matched.

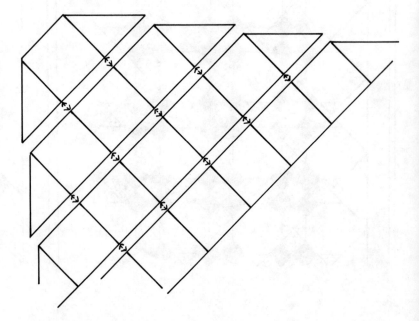

The result will be a nice straight side of the quilt.
When piecing these rows, you will discover that as a rule, each row has either two more or two less squares in the row.

Corners

The corners on these odd-numbered diagonally set quilts use a triangle that is different than those used for the setting triangles on the sides.

Whether or not you are floating the setting triangles, an easy way to do these corners without figuring the exact size would be to:

Add an inch to the finished block measurement and cut two squares that size.

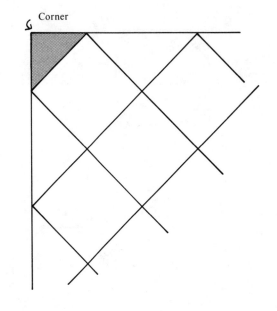

Corner

Then cut them diagonally. This will yield triangles that are too large, but sew them on anyway.

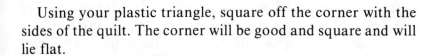

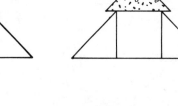

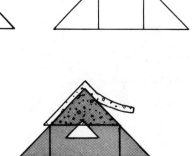

Using your plastic triangle, square off the corner with the sides of the quilt. The corner will be good and square and will lie flat.

The corners on an even-numbered diagonally set quilt are easier than on the odd ones. Use two setting triangles on the corners. You will need to know this, so you can add these eight setting triangles to the ones you planned for the sides.

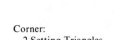

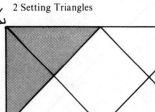

Corner:
2 Setting Triangles

NOTE: To make these setting triangles in the quilts in the pattern section, we will take large squares and cut with an X (cutting from corner to corner and then the other direction, corner to corner).

Snowball Blocks

Every quiltmaker has a favorite block they love to experiment with. I happen to be excited over the Snowball block. This simple little square, with its corners cut off, works well with other pieced blocks. It is constantly a surprise to see it used over and over in quilts.

When you find this block in books, it is usually in combination with other pieced blocks. Its function is to connect designs. It is much prettier than alternating pieced blocks with just plain blocks. The Snowball blocks extend the design and form more interesting overall patterns that the ingredients alone could not do.

When full-size templates are given, the Snowball block is an odd shape. With this shape is a triangle to be sewn onto the bias edges.

A more accurate way is to cut off the correct amount from the squares, cut the proper triangle, and then fit them exactly.

If we think of the Snowball block as a square with the corners cut off, we can cut off the right amount with the rotary cutter. To know how much to cut off, we will be making a cutting guide. This guide looks like a template, but is not used as one. I refer to this guide as a SPEEDY.

The Snowball cutting guide is made by drawing the finished triangle that will be sewn onto the corners, adding the seam allowance along the two shorter edges, and removing $1/4$" from the diagonal edge.

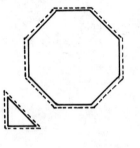

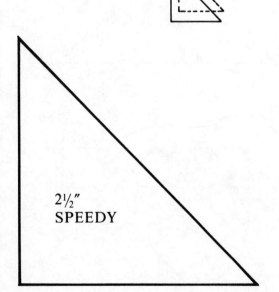

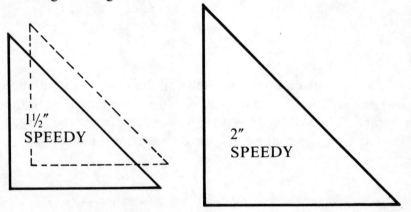

The three sizes of SPEEDYs used in the pattern section of the book are drawn here. You can just transfer them onto plastic. I do think it is important to know how to make one though, as you may find other designs that use this technique. Cutting the excess off a shape is a technique that goes beyond the Snowball blocks.

You really need to make this guide of plastic. It needs to be thick enough to stop the ruler at the proper position.

The size of the Snowball block and the size of its corner triangles are determined by the block it is going to be paired with. In the Evening Star quilt, we will be taking off ¼ of the side measurement. For example, if you were using an 8″ finished Snowball square, you would use the 2″ SPEEDY to cut off the corners. In the Snowball and Twist quilts, we will be removing ⅓ of the side measurement. For example, for a 6″ finished block, use the 2″ SPEEDY, and for a 7½″ finished Snowball block, use the 2½″ SPEEDY.

Around the Twist   Evening Star

Remember, the Snowball squares are cut from strips. Cut strips, fold in several layers and cut into squares.

I stack these squares in at least four layers, set the guide into the corner, and push against it with the mini-ruler. This tells the ruler where you need to cut. Move the guide out of the way and cut along the ruler.

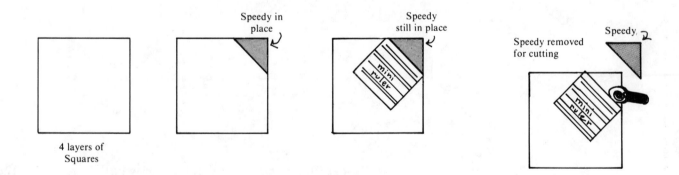

4 layers of
Squares

Speedy in place

Speedy still in place

Speedy removed for cutting

Speedy

To know which SPEEDY to use, determine the size of the triangle that will be sewn back on. If you are adding a 2″ triangle, then use the 2″ SPEEDY, and so on.

By having the control gained by cutting off the corners, you can determine how many corners are cut off. Sometimes only two or three corners will be cut off in order to get the design to float.

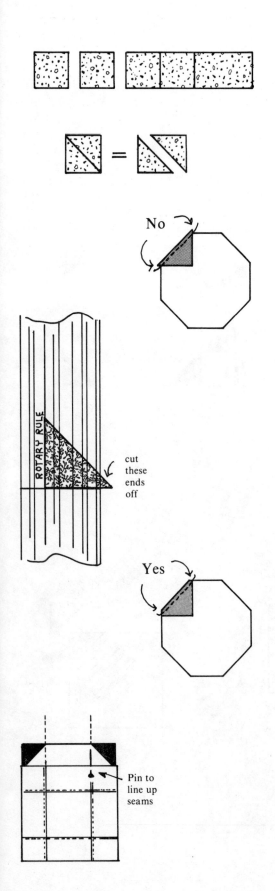

The corners to be sewn onto the Snowball Squares are loose triangles that we covered earlier (finished size of the triangle plus $\frac{7}{8}$″ squares cut diagonally).

These triangles, though, are pointed and if you were to use them now, you would have to guess somewhat to get them in place. If you blunt the tips, they will fit exactly.

There is a simple way to nub them:

Take a stack of these triangles. Using the ruler, measure the finished size of the triangle plus $\frac{1}{2}$″. Then cut the excess off. Do this on both points. These nubbed triangles then fit the Snowball block exactly.

The $\frac{1}{4}$″ seam will result in a perfect square when these are ironed open.

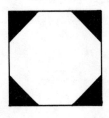

Be careful when sewing these Snowball blocks to other pieced blocks, because you will have an angled seam meeting a straight seam.

These marvelous crib quilts, sewn in pastel colors, machine piece quickly and easily using the template-free method. Snowball, left, 40" x 48½", alternates the Snowball and Nine Patch blocks.

Around the Twist, below, 39 x 47½", is executed in two colors and alternates the Twist block with a Snowball block. Decorative machine quilting adds interest to both quilts.

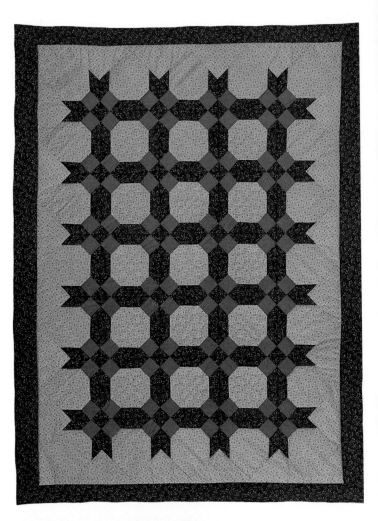

The design of these Snowball quilts is enhanced by the diagonal set and pointed edges of the blocks. This is achieved by selectively cutting the corners from the Snowball blocks. Snowball, right, 49'' x 66'', is done in browns and blues.

The large Snowball quilt, below, 86'' x 107'', shows off decorative machine quilting.

This Snowball Scrap Quilt, 52½" x 67½", uses random scraps within a pieced border. The consistent background fabric of the Snowball blocks unifies the quilt; there is a heart design machine quilted in each center.

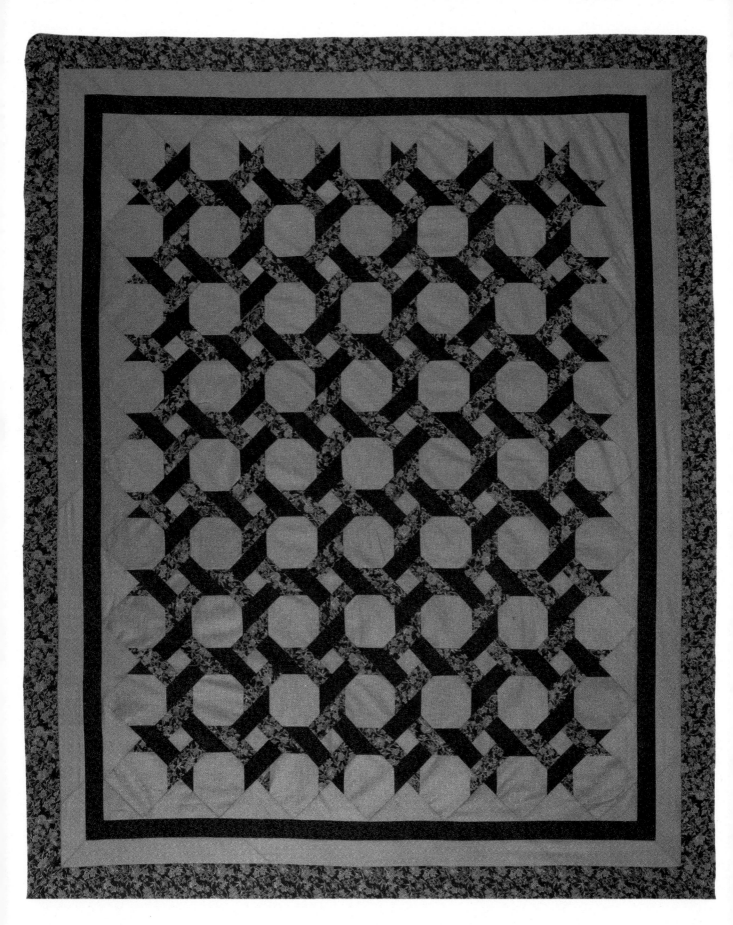

Wonderful contrast is shown in this Around the Twist design, 94'' x 115'', using a light gray background accented with a black print and a floral print.

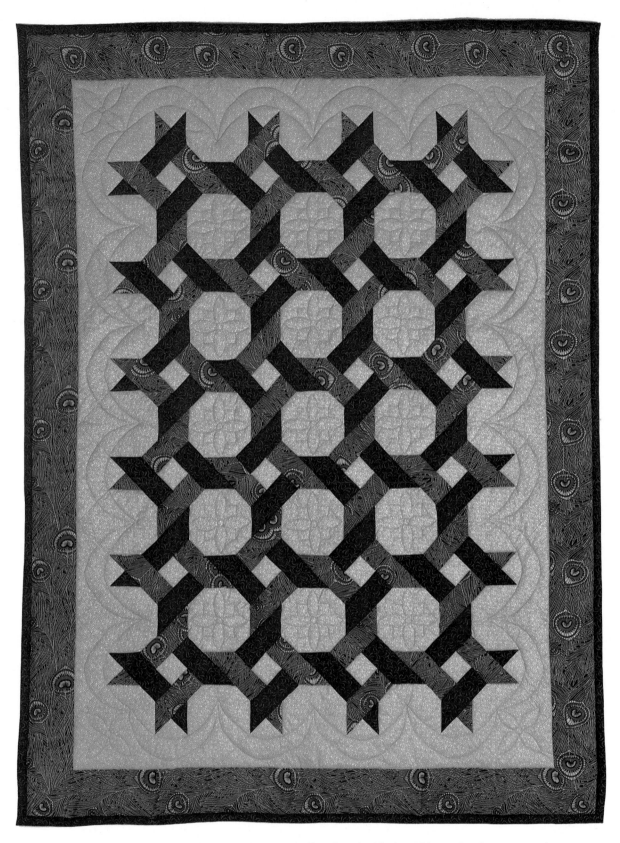

Around the Twist, 49" x 66", alternates the Snowball and Twist blocks. This version features a unique combination of a dark fabric and batik print against a beige print background. The print effectively shows the swag design that has been machine quilted.

This Around the Twist crib quilt, 39" x 47½", done in Amish colors, has a strong graphic design.

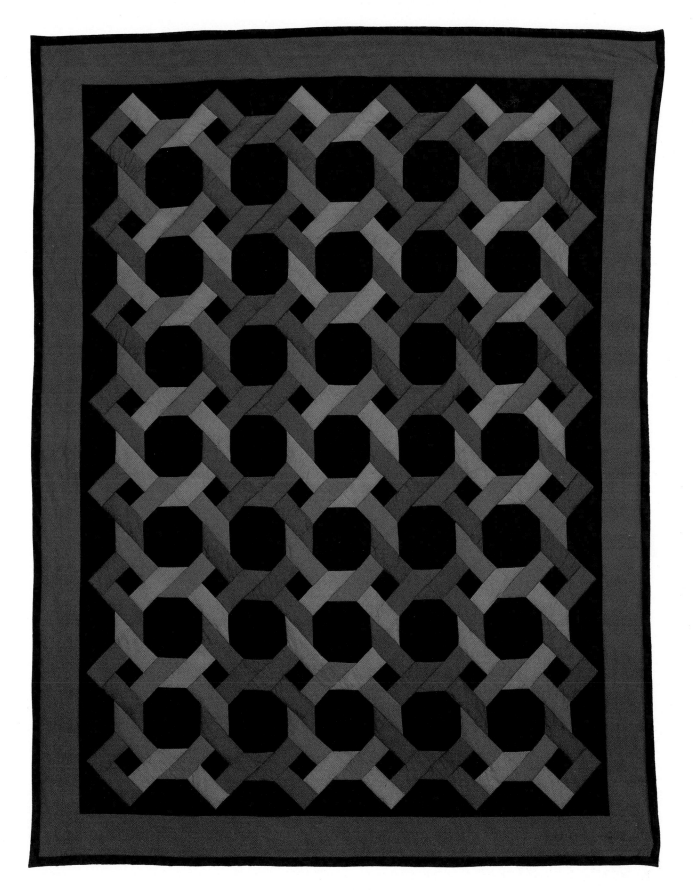

The five-color version of Around the Twist, 59'' x 76'', is not as difficult as it appears. There are two different Twist blocks that alternate with the Snowball blocks. Although they use the same fabrics, they are not sewn in the same order.

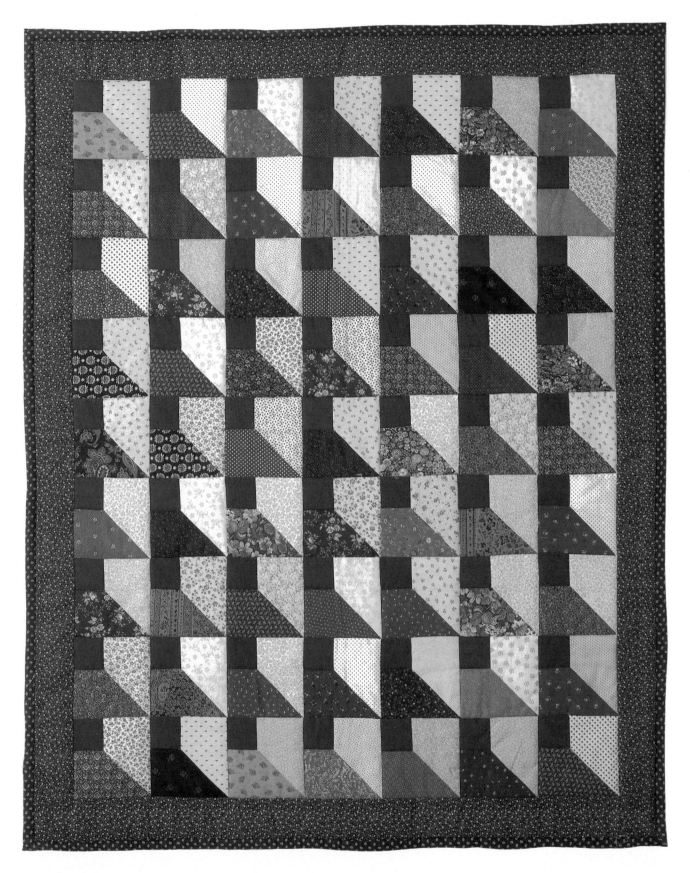

Attic Windows, 40" x 49", is one of the advanced applications possible with this template-free method of quilt construction. This scrap quilt features varying light and dark fabrics in the same position.

Fabric Choices

Since we are going to "cut and go", there are some fabrics that will be ideal and some that may give you grief. If you do a few minutes of planning ahead of time, you won't be disappointed when the quilt is finished.

Random overall patterns that do not seem to have any particular direction are wonderful choices. Big prints and paisleys are marvelous as they fill up space and seem to have something different happening all the time.

Directional fabrics are poor choices. These are ones that have a flower or figure printed in one or two directions only. If you cut these and turn them around freely when sewing, they come back to haunt you. Stripes are good for borders but hard to work with when using the rotary cutter.

I think the most important thing to keep in mind when selecting fabrics is the scale of the prints used. A variety of fabric scales results in a much more interesting quilt. Select large and small, dots, and vinelike prints. I watch people suffer over fabric selections, and then they usually go back to their first choice. I think it is rather like reading a recipe. You can usually tell by the ingredients whether you will like the finished result.

If selecting fabric is a chore, here are some simple tips we give in our shop.

1. Look at your pattern and decide how many fabrics will be needed, then find a fabric that you really want to work with. If it has more than one color in it, the fabrics will help pick themselves.

2. Keep in mind that monochromatic quilts are the hardest to choose. You will mostly be working with shading, and for beginners this is difficult.

3. Don't over-coordinate. Sometimes a fabric can look altogether different at close range than it does when you view it from farther back. A shade variation will sometimes give the finished quilt the punch it needs.

4. Reverse prints can make a calm design quite busy, since they are the same scale. Look for another fabric with the same color but a larger or smaller print.

Good Choices

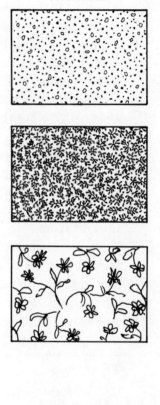

Poor Choices

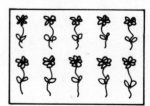

41

Yardage

The question most often asked in quiltmaking is "How much fabric will I need?" Most of us love patterns or books that answer that question for us. I have tried in this book to give you yardages for more than one size of each design. However, it is important for you to know how to figure yardage on your own, as you may wish to enlarge or reduce the size of these quilts.

The first thing to keep in mind is the width of the fabric. Despite what the manufacturers print on the end of the bolt (usually 44/45"), those of us who work with many brands know not to plan with this width. After discarding the selvage and the manufacturer's name (many put them in as far as ½"), you really only have about 42" of usable fabric left. Think of fabric as being 42" wide to avoid disappointment.

Once you convert to these techniques, you will begin to think of fabric differently. Since most of the cutting will be cross-grain, think of how many units you can cut from a strip of fabric 42" wide. For example, you can plan on cutting fourteen 3" squares from one 3" wide strip. However, you could only get two 15" squares from a 15" wide strip.

To calculate your yardage, first decide what shapes you need to cut. Figure out the size and the number of units needed. Take the number needed and divide by the number you can get from one strip. The resulting number will tell you how many strips to cut. Take the width of the strip and multiply it by the number of strips needed. If you divide that by 36" you will know how many yards to buy.

To help you figure your own yardage:	STRIP WIDTH	NUMBER OF SQUARES	STRIP WIDTH	NUMBER OF SQUARES
	2	21	11	3
	2.5	16	11.5	3
	3	14	12	3
	3.5	12	12.5	3
	4	10	13	3
	4.5	9	13.5	3
	5	8	14	3
	5.5	7	14.5	2
	6	7	15	2
	6.5	6	15.5	2
	7	6	16	2
	7.5	5	16.5	2
	8	5	17	2
	8.5	4	17.5	2
	9	4	18	2
	9.5	4	18.5	2
	10	4	19	2
	10.5	4	19.5	2

When I calculate yardage for triangles, I imagine that two triangles put together equal a square approximately 1″ larger than I want the finished triangle. To figure how many 3″ finished triangles I can get, I figure how many 4″ squares I can get from a 4″ wide strip and divide by two.

Plan to buy more fabric than you actually need. This bit of insurance may save several trips back to the store. You might accidently cut a strip incorrectly and be short the required units. When working on a large project over a long period of time, I have been known to lose parts and I need to recut. One-fourth yard of extra material is cheap insurance.

In planning yardage for borders, calculate cutting the width cross-grain. However, if it is a 7″ or wider border, I usually buy the length of the quilt and cut the borders lengthwise. There is really less waste. The leftovers make great bindings.

When you add the amount you will need for piecing and the amount you will need for the borders, sometimes the sum is the length of the quilt or longer. In this case, you can cut your borders lengthwise first, and set aside. Then cut the rest of the yardage for piecing.

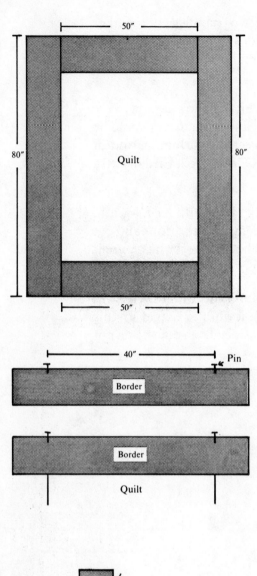

Borders

Over the years, I have observed quiltmakers doing wonderful work piecing their quilts, only to undo it when they put the borders on. Many people just take a strip of fabric and sew it on the edge of their quilt and then cut it off. Many times they put different amounts on each time they sew, creating real problems.

The opposite sides of a quilt should be the same measurement when the borders have been applied. This is done by measuring the quilt prior to sewing on borders. Once the measurement has been established, precut the borders to match. If you are not mitering, you can cut them accurately, matching them to the quilt at each end and the middle, then sewing them on. Start with two opposite sides, and then the other two sides.

If you are mitering, place a pin where the border measurement begins and ends and leave an adequate amount beyond the pin to allow for mitering. Using the pins at the ends also ensures that the proper amount of border is added to your quilt.

You really want the quilt to be squared when finished, so it will hang right on the bed or in competition.

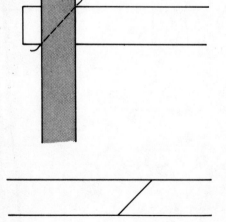

In calculating my quilts, I try to figure the entire quilt. The borders are calculated to be cut cross-grain and then pieced. If they are pieced on an angle, the seam will hardly be noticed. Take the strips, overlap into an L, and then stitch from the outside edge to the the outside edge.

If one of the fabrics in the pieced area will be repeated in the border, these two yardages may add up to an amount that will allow you to cut the borders lengthwise, eliminating the seams. Sometimes there is enough left over from piecing the backing that the borders can be cut lengthwise as well. For example, in lap quilts, if you bought two lengths of the quilt, the borders could be gotten out of the backing fabric. Sometimes it helps to plan ahead.

Borders are very important to the look of your finished quilt. They should frame the quilt and not distract from it.

STRIPES make great borders. They can spice up an otherwise boring quilt. If you are putting them on a square piece, establish where the center of each side will be. Usually, some part of a design will be a good starting point. Next, measure what you need and set it up for mitering as mentioned earlier. If the quilt is square and four sides have the same part of the design at the midpoint, then all four corners will look the same.

If you are putting a stripe onto a rectangle and you still want all four corners to repeat the same part of the design, you will need to figure the repeat of the design in the stripe and make the quilt mathematically compatible. Treat the stripe fabric as if it were a pieced border. Sometimes a plain border can be added to the quilt before the stripe. The width of this plain border can be used to make the stripe compatible.

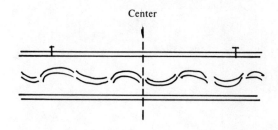

Center

How to Miter

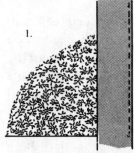

1.

Begin and end ¼″ from the edges.

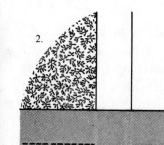

2.

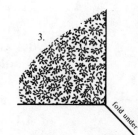

3.

Fold under strip coming from left. Line up inside cut edges.

fold under

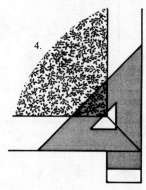

4.

Check to be sure you are square, using your triangle. Then press.

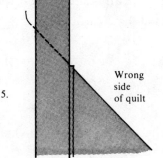

5.

Wrong side of quilt

Stitch in crease to previous stitching lines.

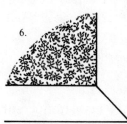

6.

Check the front to be sure there is no problem, then trim seam to ¼″.

45

Finishing Your Quilt

Nothing can really replace the wonderful look of hand quilting. However, it is not the best choice for all quilts and it is very time consuming. If you are just going to outline your piecing, why not do it on the machine?

Crib quilts and heavily used quilts which will be washed over and over are ideal choices to machine quilt. The more you quilt on the machine, the more comfortable you will become. Most of the quilts in this book have been machine quilted. Some include freehand machine quilting using a darning foot on the machine. The following tips will enable you to machine quilt with any standard sewing machine.

Backing

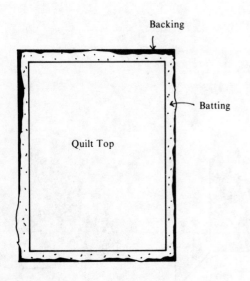

Batting

Quilt Top

Layering

Measure your quilt. The size of your finished top will determine the size backing and batting you will need. You should plan the back and batting to be 2″ to 3″ larger than the finished top on all sides. I love backings cut from busy prints for machine-quilted quilts. After they are quilted the actual stitches do not show, just the outline of the design. These busy prints are excellent choices for inexperienced machine quilters, since they help to conceal work that is "less than perfect".

The backing may be pieced with horizontal or vertical seams; they won't be seen once it is quilted. Just before layering, give it one last pressing to remove any remaining fold lines and to ensure that the seaming is flat.

Horizontal Piecing   Vertical Piecing

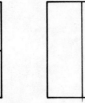

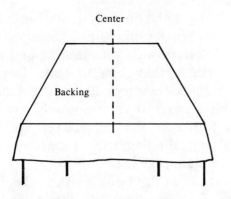

Center

Backing

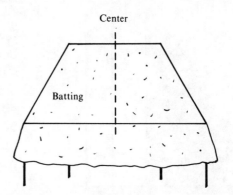

Center

Batting

Lay out the back of your quilt on a table wrong side up. The floor is not a good choice, since you usually have to crawl onto it and things will surely shift. Use a table pad to protect your dining room table. A ping pong table or long tables also work well.

Spread your batting over the backing, smooth and pull out any remaining folds.

Place the quilt on top, centering it on the back. Check all four sides to see that there is adequate back and batting. Reach under the batting and tug the back to pull out any waves made by layering. If you don't, you may quilt the tucks in. Smooth out the top with your hands, checking for any odd bumps from either the batting or the back.

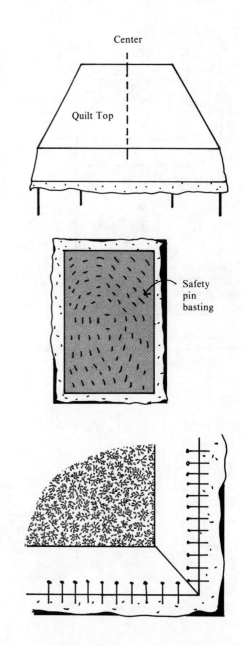

Center

Quilt Top

Safety pin basting

Baste your quilt with safety pins. A size 2 safety pin works great. It is not too small to catch all layers, but is not so large that it makes big holes in the quilt. More and more quilt shops are carrying these. This system works for hand quilting as well. The safety pin method of basting holds the layers secure. There isn't the play in the three layers that you often find in hand basting. There are no threads to snag and pull out, and the speed in assembling is wonderful. The pinning should be at frequent intervals. You should not be able to put your hand down without hitting a pin. Every 4″ is not too close together. The more you put in, the easier you can handle your quilt. I put a quilt on my 17-year-old son's bed before I could find time to quilt it and he wondered about the pins. I told him it was a "punk" quilt and he snuggled right under it. One of my students said her mother-in-law asked if quilters were doing that now instead of tying those little bows. The pins are bound to cause comments from those who have never seen safety pin basting.

Straight pin the outside edge perpendicular to the edge of the quilt at about 1½″ intervals. As soon as the inside of your quilt is secured, the outside wants to flip up and ripple. This fluff has to be held in place.

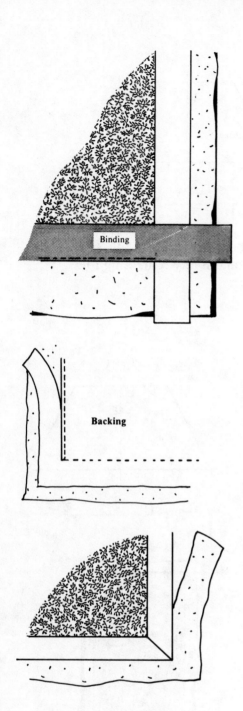

Binding

Binding

At this time I go ahead and bind my quilts. Since I feel very secure with the safety pin basting, I finish the edge so that the batting does not interfere with the machine quilting. I use straight bindings rather than bias to make larger, fatter bindings. On large quilts, these look like piping. Bindings can be single or double layered. If you want only one layer, cut binding strips 2½" to 3" wide. For double layered bindings, cut binding strips 5½" wide. Binding strips are cut cross-grain and pieced together at a slant (like the borders).

All the quilt patterns in this book give you the number of strips needed for single bindings. Be sure to increase the yardage purchased to cut wider strips for double bindings.

Even if I do not miter all borders, I miter my bindings. It makes for a more pleasing corner. Sew the bindings on through all layers.

Backing

Remove the straight pins, miter the corners, and trim excess backing (not the batting) away about ¼" from the stitching you just completed.

Open the binding out and trim the batting even with that outside edge. This excess batting will be folded in when the binding is brought to the back.

Even though I do everything else on the machine, I prefer to finish the bindings on the quilt back by hand. For gently rounded bindings, turn under ¼" of the raw edge and bring that fold just past the stitching line on the back. Sew with an applique stitch or blind stitch. This stitching should not be visible.

Handling the Corners

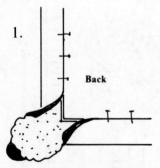

1.

Back

Pin from both directions.

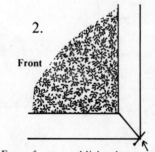

2.

Front

From front establish where corner will turn. Place a pin. **Pin**

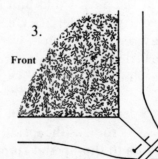

3.

Front

Cut away excess binding and batting ¼" away from pin.

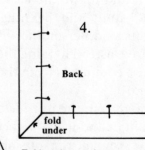

4.

Back

fold under

Fold under a miter at corner and stitch.

48

Machine Quilting

To determine where to quilt, examine the design of the quilt. Machine quilting is best done in the seams, so that it is not the main feature of the quilt. First break the pattern into the design blocks and stitch into seams that will highlight the design. Too much machine quilting will smash the batting down and not look pleasing. You can always add more quilting if it looks baggy when you think you are done. You should try to avoid making quilt tops look like mattress pads. When you are burying the stitching in the seams, try to sew on the side of the seam that does not have the seam allowance.

When quilting on the machine, do the worst first. I think of this as the seams that involve handling the most bulk. This is the least fun — but it gets easier with every seam. Quilt from edge to edge of the quilt. There is no need to start in the middle of the quilt. You will have to handle the most bulk with the line of stitching that goes across the quilt.

Next, machine quilt down the middle. Thereafter, all lines of stitching will have less and less bulk to handle. I have one wonderful chant that I use when quilting large quilts. I just say over and over aloud, "IT WOULD TAKE ME SIX MONTHS TO HAND QUILT THIS. IT WOULD TAKE ME SIX MONTHS TO HAND QUILT THIS. IT WOULD TAKE ME SIX MONTHS TO HAND QUILT THIS . . . ." You would be surprised at how you can push that bulk through your machine after the chant.

The real secret to my machine quilting is the control of the fluff created by the batting. The actual line that I am quilting is pinned perpendicularly with straight quilter's pins at about 2″ intervals. My palms hold down the rest. I keep my eye out for any movement of the three layers and stretch to prevent tucks.

If you are quilting designs with your sewing machine, try a darning foot, sometimes called a machine embroidery foot. This will allow you to freely move the quilt and follow a drawn design. Some machines allow you this freedom by enabling you to drop the feed dog. It takes a bit of practice to get comfortable, but wonderful results can be achieved. I recommend clear thread on open areas so that the thread is not seen. Also when I backstitch to start and stop, no thread can be seen.

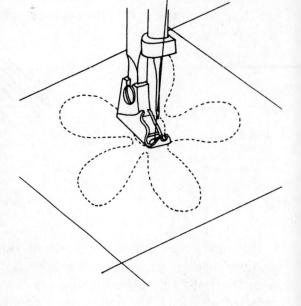

Take breaks when quilting begins to tire you. You will feel all bent over if you stay at the machine too long. I try to take at least three days to quilt a large quilt, and even then my back aches.

It is really fun to see your quilt come to life so quickly.

Advanced Applications

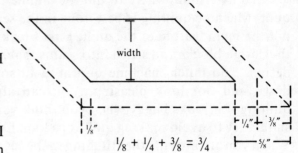

$$\frac{1}{8} + \frac{1}{4} + \frac{3}{8} = \frac{3}{4}$$

The more I work with this system, the more fun it becomes. I seem to discover something new every day.

Parallelograms

Parallelograms seem to crop up in designs I work with, so I first drafted one on graph paper. When I put the seam allowance all around, I discovered that from one cut edge to the other equaled **the side plus ¾″.**

To cut these, cut a strip equal to the width plus the ¼″ seam allowance for both sides.

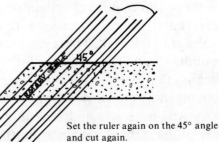

Set the ruler again on the 45° angle and cut again.

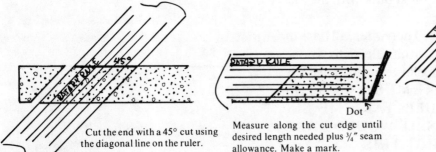

Cut the end with a 45° cut using the diagonal line on the ruler.

Measure along the cut edge until desired length needed plus ¾″ seam allowance. Make a mark.

The 45° diamonds are parallelograms.

The Lone Star quilt and other designs with these diamonds suddenly seem easier. When two or more diamonds are to be sewn together, sew strips together and then use the ruler to cut the proper angle. It is the same principle as that used in straight cuts.

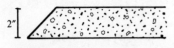

Cut desired width strips and cut a 45° point.

Set the 45° angle of the ruler until the cut angled edge lines up with the ruler's numbers that correspond with the width strip cut. No need for marking.

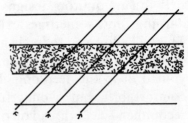

cut for sewn diamonds

Clay's Choice

If I work with a design where one particular fabric has the points consistently going in one direction, I layer the strips with the right side always facing up (so I don't cut some reversed pieces). If the design has a reverse of this shape as well, I just fold the strip so that when I cut I will get both the shape and its reverse.

50

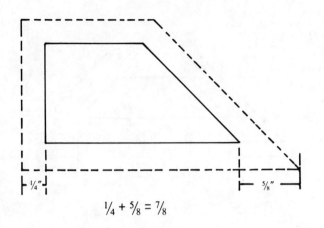

$$\frac{1}{4} + \frac{5}{8} = \frac{7}{8}$$

Trapezoids

In trapezoids (as shown here) I discovered that the same math used in half-square triangles applied here. Just add ⅞″ to the long side. I cut a strip the width of the trapezoid plus the seam allowances.

Working with four layers, clean up the left edge perpendicular with the cut edge and from that edge measure the finished edge of the long side plus ⅞″ and cut again with the 45° mark on the ruler. These fit all other shapes involved. You must be careful to see if these shapes have the point going the same direction or if they are used in both directions. This will tell you how to layer the strips. This shape is almost always used independently in designs. It usually has a triangle sewn to the pointed edge, yielding a rectangle.

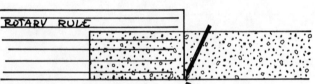

Measure and mark the finished side plus ⅞″.

Here it is sewn into an Attic Window block which has a square three-fifths the measurement of the long side.

Attic Window

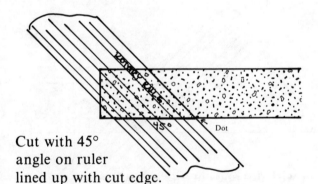

Cut with 45° angle on ruler lined up with cut edge.

Here it is sewn to two-thirds of a Nine Patch.

Shortcut to School

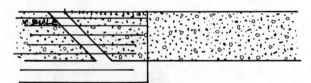

The next cut does not have to be marked. Measure the desired amount and make a straight cut.

It makes no difference what shape will be attached to this. The math still holds. Here it is sewn to a square one half the measurement of the long side.

Puss in the Corner

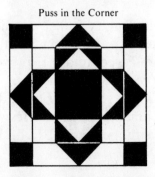

51

"Decapitated Triangles"

In shapes as used in Pineapple quilts, and blocks like Kings X, the math is already known. This shape is also very common in corners of designs and borders.

These shapes remind me of a quarter-square triangle with its tip cut off. The math is the same. You usually know the long side. **So take the measurement of the long side and add 1¼".**

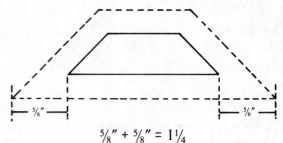

$$\frac{5}{8}'' + \frac{5}{8}'' = 1\frac{1}{4}$$

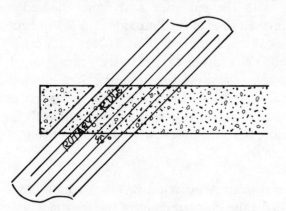

Establish the 45° angle using the ruler. Cut.

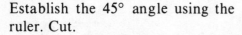

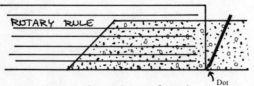

Measure along the edge of strip until you get to desired long side plus 1¼" seam allowance. Mark.

Line up ruler with dot and cut a 45° angle cut the the opposite direction.

Shadow Box

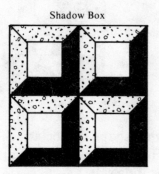

Pineapple Block

The Rotary Rule™ also has a 60° marking. Therefore, 60° shapes can also be cut with this system. Sixty-degree diamonds are quite common. However, they usually appear in blocks that require hand piecing.

As you search for more designs to use the rotary cutter, it will amaze you that so few formulas are used over and over. Have fun and go QUILT LIKE CRAZY.

Quilt Patterns

Strip Bow Quilts

This is a quilt that is set diagonally, with two blocks in the first row. As you can see, it uses two alternating blocks. These blocks are created swiftly using strips.

Large Quilt — Piecing finishes to 70" by 87". With the borders it measures 86" by 105".

This quilt calls for four fabrics. They should be chosen so that the two strongest colors are on the ends of the sewn strips. In that way, the bow is really highlighted. All strips are cut the same width. In this design they were cut 2" wide, but they could be made narrower or wider.

Fabric Requirements

Main Four Fabrics — 2 yds. each
Setting Fabric — 1½ yds.
Borders — 2¾ yds. of darker (will give you two borders and binding), 1 yd. of a medium
Backing — 6½ yds.

Cutting Requirements

Main Four Fabrics — Cut 30 strips 2" wide for strip units.
Setting Fabric — Cut 10 squares 11" from 4 strips 11" wide. Cut these with an X to yield 40 setting triangles.

For the large quilt, you will need to make 30 strip units to make 178 blocks.

Border Fabric —

1. From dark fabric cut 17 strips 3½″ wide for 1st and 3rd borders. Also cut 10 strips 2½″ wide for binding.

2. For medium fabric cut 7 strips 2½″ wide for 3 sides of 2nd border and 2 strips 4½″ wide for top.

Piecing and Assembly

1. First sew the 4 colors of strips together to make a unit. Both blocks are created from the same unit of strips. Each unit will yield 6 blocks. Press all seams in one sewn unit in one direction. Half the units are pressed in one direction and the other half will be pressed in the opposite direction.

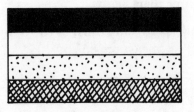

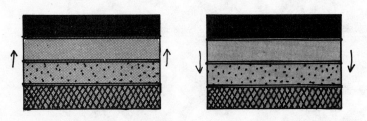

Now take 2 sets of strips that are pressed in opposite directions and place them with right sides together matching colors. You will find that the seam allowances are now going in opposite directions, reducing the need to line them up when sewn. Measure the width of the sewn unit and use that measurement to cut the strip into squares (they should measure 6½″). Cut these squares with 1 diagonal cut. The resulting triangles are lined up ready to sew. Sew down the long side and press. You will find two types of blocks which we will alternate in the design.

2. Join the blocks according to the diagram into rows. Join the rows.

3. Add borders.

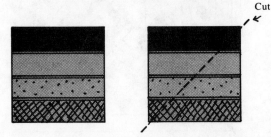

Cut

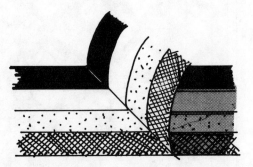

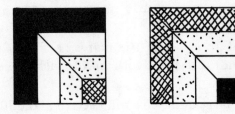

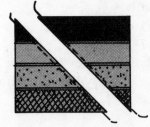

54

Lap Quilt — Piecing finishes to 38″ by 53″. With borders, it will finish to 46″ by 61″.

Fabric Requirements

Main Four Fabrics — ¾ yd. each
Setting Fabric — 1 yd.
Backing, Borders, and Binding — 4 yd.

Cutting Requirements

Main Four Fabrics — Cut 10 strips 2″ wide for strip units.
Setting Fabric — Cut 6 squares 11″ from 2 strips 11″ wide. Cut with an X to yield 24 setting triangles.

Borders and Binding — After piecing back, cut 4 strips 4½″ wide for t' borders and 4 strips 2½″ wide for binding lengthwise from the extra width.

For the lap quilt, you will need to make 10 strip units to make 58 blocks.

Crib Quilt — Piecing area finishes to 32½" by 48".
With borders it will finish to 38½" by 54".

Yardage Requirements

Main Four Fabrics — ½ yd. of each
Setting Fabric — ¾ yd. (This can be added to
   one of the above.)
Borders — ¾ yd.
Binding — ½ yd.
Backing — 1¾ yd.

Cutting Requirements

Main Four Fabrics — Cut 7 strips 2" wide for strip
   units.
Setting Fabric — Cut 5 squares 11" from 2 strips
   11" wide. Cut these with an X to yield 20 setting
   triangles. These will float the design.
Border Fabric — Cut 5 strips 3½" wide.
Binding — Cut 5 strips 2½" wide.

For the crib quilt, you will need 7 strip units to
make 38 blocks.

A large Strip Bow quilt, 86'' x 105'', is comprised of two alternating blocks. The diagonal set and the subtle color scheme contribute to the overall design.

The Strip Bow quilt, right, 38½" x 54", is done in strong primary colors that will brighten any nursery.

Judy's Star, below, 41" x 54", is a wall hanging executed in a more restful color scheme. Six pieced stars and delicate hand quilting are framed by a pieced border.

Judy's Star, 75'' x 96'', is a large quilt done in deep solid colors. This graphic design features a solid color border with stars falling on the pillow area.

59

Kris's Three Patch, 82'' x 102'', is a three color design made from the same block. Varying the position and placement of the blocks results in this wonderful overall design.

This blue, beige and rust variation of Kris's Three Patch, 57'' x 74'', effectively uses three subtle prints.

Devil's Claw, 72" x 102", is comprised of four small Evening Star blocks. A wide border surrounds the blocks below the Evening Star design on the pillow area.

Evening Star, left, 72"x104", combines the Evening Star and Snowball blocks in a brown color scheme to create an overall design. A flower is machine quilted inside each Snowball block.

The Evening Star wall hanging, below, 40" x 40", has a border of striped fabric which effectively frames the machine quilted Evening Star and Snowball blocks.

Nine Patch of Nine Patches, right, 47"
x 59", is a striking quilt with its reverse
color scheme and detailed machine
quilting.

The same quilt top is shown below in
red, with the light and dark color placement reversed.

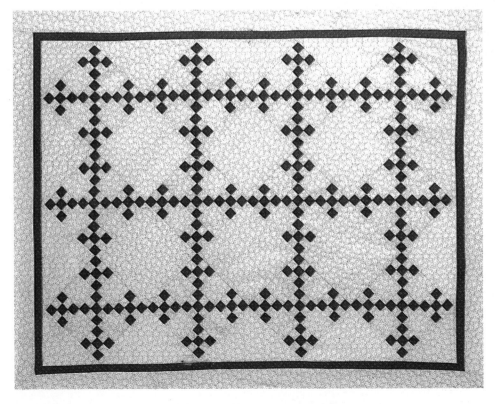

Nine Patch of Nine Patches

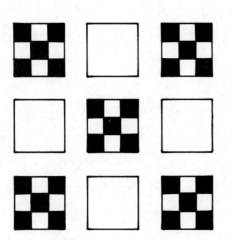

Nine Patch blocks with alternate plain blocks.

The design unit used in this quilt is a 9" Nine Patch block made up of smaller Nine Patch blocks alternated with plain blocks. These Nine Patch blocks are made from strips (refer to the techniques section to see the best way to piece Nine Patch blocks). There are three sets of sewn strips that are consistently pressed toward the same fabric. These three sets of sewn strips are referred to as a setup. Each setup in this quilt will yield twenty-eight small Nine Patch blocks. One setup will look like this:

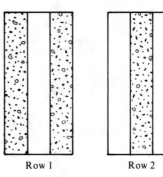

Row 1   Row 2   Row 3

Large Quilt — Piecing finishes 78″ by 91″. With borders the quilt finishes 84″ by 97″.

Fabric Requirements

Background — 6½ yd.
Main — 4 yd. (2 yd. for piecing and 2 yd. for borders and binding)
Backing — 6 yd.

Cutting Requirements

Background

1. Cut 32 strips 1½″ wide for small Nine Patches.

2. Cut 14 strips 3½″ wide into 168 squares 3½″.

3. Cut 8 strips 9½″ wide into 30 squares 9½″.

4. Cut 6 squares 15″ from 3 strips 15″ wide. Cut these with an X to yield 22 setting triangles. These will float the design.

5. Cut 2 squares 10″ once diagonally for the corners.

Main

1. Cut 40 strips 1½″ wide for small Nine Patches.

2. Cut 10 strips 3½″ wide for borders.

3. Cut 10 strips 2½″ wide for binding.

Piecing and Assembly

1. Piece the 1½″ wide strips together into 8 setups.

2. Cut into 1½″ wide segments and sew 210 small Nine Patch blocks.

3. Alternate these small Nine Patch blocks with the 3½″ background squares to make the 42 larger Nine Patch blocks.

4. Join the larger blocks with plain blocks and setting triangles into rows. Join the rows.

5. Add the borders.

Small Quilt — Piecing finishes 39" by 51". With borders it finishes 47" by 59".

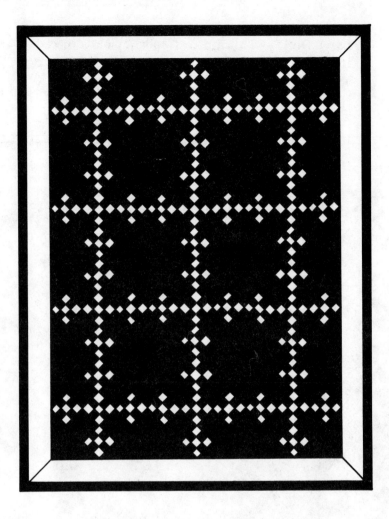

Fabric Requirements

Background — 3¾ yd. (3 yd. for piecing, ¾ yd. for borders)

Main — 1¾ yd. (¾ yd. for piecing, 1 yd. for border and binding)

Backing — 3 yd. pieced crosswise

Cutting Requirements

Background

1. Cut 12 strips 1½" wide for small Nine Patch setups.

2. Cut 4 strips 3½" wide into 48 squares 3½".

3. Cut 2 strips 9½" wide into 6 squares 9½".

4. Cut 2 strips 15" wide into 3 squares 15". Cut these with an X to yield 10 setting triangles. These will float the design.

5. Cut 2 squares 10" once diagonally for the corners.

6. Cut 7 strips 3½" wide for the 2nd border.

Main

1. Cut 15 strips 1½" wide for small Nine Patch setups.

2. Cut 5 strips 1½" wide for the 1st border.

3. Cut 7 strips 2½" wide for binding.

Piecing and Assembly

1. Piece the 1½" strips according to the diagram to make 3 setups.

2. Cut into 1½" segments and make 60 small Nine Patches.

3. Alternate these small Nine Patches with the 3½" background squares to make the 12 larger Nine Patch blocks.

4. Join the larger blocks with the large plain squares and setting triangles to form the rows. Join the rows.

5. Add borders.

Kris's Three Patch

Large Quilt — This illustration will yield a pieced area approximately 64″ by 84″. With the two borders the quilt finishes to 82″ by 102″.

Fabric Requirements

Light — 2¾ yds. (1¾ yds. for piecing, 1 yd. for borders)

Medium — 3½ yds. (1¾ yds. for piecing, 1¾ yds. for borders)

Dark — 4 yds. (3 yds. for piecing, 1 yd. for binding)

Backing — 6¼ yds.

Cutting Requirements

Light —
1. Cut 18 strips 3" wide for blocks.
2. Cut 8 strips 4" wide for border.

Medium —
1. Cut 6 strips 3" wide for blocks.
2. Cut 6 strips 5½" wide for blocks.
3. Cut 9 strips 5½" wide for 2nd border.

Dark —
1. Cut 6 strips 3" wide for blocks.
2. Cut 6 strips 5½" wide for blocks.
3. Cut 3 strips 13" wide into 7 squares 13". Cut these with an X to yield 28 setting triangles. These will float the design.
4. Cut 10 strips 2½" wide for binding.

Piecing and Assembly

1. Piece strips together into 6 setups. A setup looks like the illustration below, and yields 14 blocks. It is simpler than the setup for a Nine Patch, yet subcut the same. Sew the strips and be consistent with the pressing. Subcut with 3" cuts and piece 82 blocks.

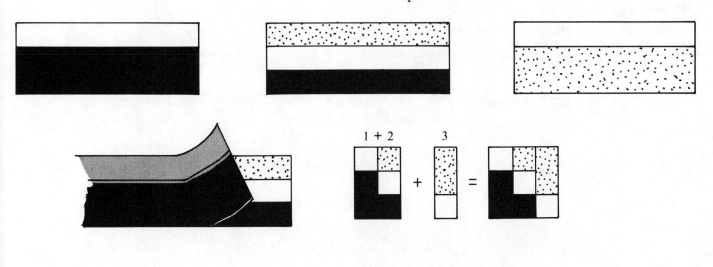

2. Piece blocks together according to the diagram. Join rows.
3. Add borders.

Lap Quilt — Piecing finishes approximately 51″ by 68″. With borders, the quilt finishes 57″ by 74″.

The lap quilt is assembled the same as the larger quilt. The sizes of the pieces of the strips and setting triangles are different. One setup will yield 16 blocks, but you will still need 6 setups.

Fabric Requirements

Light — 1½ yd.
Medium (blue) — 2½ yd.
Dark (rust) — 3 yd. (1½ yd. for piecing, 1½ yd. for border and binding)
Backing — 5 yd. (You can get your borders and binding out of the leftovers if you plan ahead.)

Cutting Requirements

Light —   Cut 18 strips 2½″ wide.
Medium — 1. Cut 6 strips 2½″ wide.
               2. Cut 6 strips 4½″ wide.
               3. Cut 7 strips 3½″ wide for borders.
               4. Cut 8 strips 2½″ wide for binding.

NOTE: If cutting border and binding lengthwise from pieced back, cut only 4 strips of each.

Dark —   1. Cut 6 strips 2½″ wide.
               2. Cut 6 strips 4½″ wide.
               3. Cut 7 squares 11″ from 3 strips 11″ wide. Cut with an X to yield 28 setting triangles. This will float the design.

Piecing and Assembly

Same as larger quilt except you will be making 2½″ subcuts.

Snowball Quilt

This quilt is simply Nine Patch blocks alternated with the Snowball block discussed earlier in the techniques section. What enhances this design is setting it diagonally and being selective when cutting off the corners of the snowball block with the SPEEDY. If all corners are not cut off from the blocks forming the outside of the pieced area, the design tends to float before the borders are put on.

Large Quilt — The pieced area finishes to 73½″ by 94½″. With borders the quilt finishes 86″ by 107″.

71

Fabrics Required

Background — 4½ yds.

Main — 5 yds. (3¼ yds. for piecing, 1¾ yds. for border)

Accent — 3¼ yds. (1¾ yds. for piecing, 1½ yds. for border and binding)

Backing — 6½ yds.

Cutting Requirements

Background

1. Cut 13 strips 8″ wide into 63 squares 8″. Then using a 2½″ SPEEDY cut 4 corners off from 35 of these and cut 2 corners off from 4, and only 3 off from 24 of these 8″ blocks.

2. Cut 3 strips 12″ wide into 7 squares 12″. Cut these squares with an X yielding 28 setting triangles. These will not float.

3. Cut 2 squares 8½″ with 1 diagonal cut for the 4 corner triangles.

Main

1. Cut 20 strips 3″ wide to make setups for Nine Patch blocks.

2. Cut 10 strips 3⅜″ wide into 110 squares 3⅜″. Cut these squares into triangles. You will need 220 for the Snowball blocks.

3. Cut 11 strips 4½″ wide for 2nd border.

Accent

1. Cut 16 strips 3″ wide for the Nine Patch blocks.

2. Cut 21 strips 2½″ wide for 1st border and binding.

Piecing and Assembly

1. Sew the 3″ strips of main and accent fabrics into 4 setups for the Nine Patch blocks. They will look like this:

Refer to the section on piecing Nine Patch blocks from strips. You will need 48 Nine Patch blocks for this quilt.

2. Add the triangles of the main fabric to the Snowball blocks.

3. Piece into rows and then join the rows.

4. Add the corners last.

5. Sew on borders.

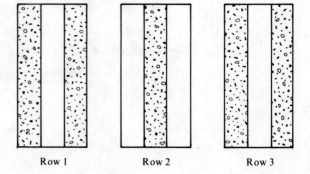

Row 1   Row 2   Row 3

Lap Quilt — Piecing finishes 42½″ by 59½″. With borders, quilt finishes to 49″ by 66″.

Fabric Requirements

Background — 2¼ yd.

Main — 2¼ yd. (1¼ yd. for piecing, 1 yd. for border)

Accent — 1½ yd. (¾ yd. for piecing, ¾ yd. for binding)

Backing — 3 yd. (pieced crosswise)

Cutting Requirements

Background

1. Cut 6 strips 6½″ wide into 35 squares 6½″. Using a 2″ SPEEDY, cut 4 corners off 15 squares, cut 3 corners off 16, and cut 2 corners off 4 squares.

2. Cut 2 strips 10″ wide into 5 squares 10″. Cut these with an X to yield 20 setting triangles. This will float the design.

3. Cut 2 squares 7″ diagonally to yield the 4 corners.

Main

1. Cut 10 strips 2½″ wide for the setups to make the Nine Patch blocks.

2. Cut 5 strips 2⅞″ wide into 58 squares 2⅞″. Cut these squares diagonally to yield 116 triangles for the Snowball blocks.

3. Cut 7 strips 3½″ wide for the border.

Accent

1. Cut 8 strips 2½″ wide for the Nine Patch blocks.

2. Cut 7 strips 2½″ wide for the binding.

Piecing and Assembly

1. Sew the 2½″ wide strips of the main and accent fabrics into 2 Nine Patch setups. Subcut and assemble 24 Nine Patch blocks.

2. Add the triangles of the main fabric to the Snowball blocks.

3. Piece into rows, join rows.

4. Add borders.

Crib Quilt — Piecing finishes 34″ by 42½″. With borders the quilt will finish 40″ by 48½″.

Fabrics Required

Background — 1½ yds.

Main — 1½ yds. (¾ yd. for piecing, ¾ yd. for border)

Accent — 1 yd. (½ yd. for piecing, ½ yd. for binding)

Backing — 1½ yds.

Cutting Requirements

Background

1. Cut 4 strips 6½″ wide into 20 squares 6½″. Then cut 4 corners off 6, cut 2 corners off 4, and cut 3 corners off 10 of these squares.

2. Cut 1 strip 10″ wide into 4 squares 10″. Cut these with an X to yield 14 setting triangles. These will not float design.

3. Cut 2 squares 7″ diagonally to yield the 4 corners.

Main

1. Cut 5 strips 2½″ wide for the setups to make the Nine Patch blocks.

2. Cut 3 strips 2⅞″ wide into 31 squares 2⅞″. Cut these squares diagonally to yield 62 loose triangles.

3. Cut 5 strips 3½″ wide for border.

Accent

1. Cut 4 strips 2½″ wide for the Nine Patch blocks.

2. Cut 5 strips 2½″ wide for binding.

Piecing and Assembly

1. Sew the 2½″ strips of the main and accent fabrics into 1 Nine Patch setup. Subcut and assemble 12 Nine Patch blocks.

2. Add the triangles of the main fabric to the Snowball blocks.

3. Piece into rows; join rows.

4. Add borders.

Because this quilt uses random scraps, we will not piece this in strips. I have tried it and the same combinations were appearing over and over. I love the real hodge podge look. The squares can be cut from several strips stacked. I try to cut four to six squares at a time.

The Nine Patch squares are made from 3″ cut squares and the Snowball blocks are 8″ squares cut from background fabric. All four corners are then cut off with the 2½″ SPEEDY. Corner triangles are cut from 3⅜″ squares cut diagonally.

HINT: If you use a different group of scraps for the triangles, you won't have the same fabrics touching each other when the blocks are joined.

The only fabric you will need a lot of is the background for the Snowball blocks.

REMEMBER: Out of every 3″ strip you cut, you will get 14 squares.

For a **crib quilt** measuring 37½″ by 52½″ (5 by 7 blocks) you will need to cut 162 loose 3″ squares sewn into 18 Nine Patch blocks, 68 corner triangles, and 17 squares 8″ from 4 strips 8″ wide (1 yd. background).

For a **lap quilt** measuring 52½″ by 67½″ (7 by 9 blocks) you will need 288 loose 3″ squares sewn into 32 Nine Patch blocks, 124 corner triangles, and 31 squares 8″ from 7 strips 8″ wide (1¾ yd. background).

For a **twin quilt** measuring 67½″ by 97½″ (7 by 13 blocks) you will need 414 loose 3″ squares sewn into 46 Nine Patch blocks, 180 corner triangles, and 45 squares 8″ from 9 strips 8″ wide (2¼ yd. background).

For a **full- or queen-size** quilt measuring 82½″ by 112½″ (11 by 15 blocks) you will need 747 loose 3″ squares sewn into 83 Nine Patch blocks, 328 corner triangles, and 82 squares 8″ from 17 strips 8″ wide (4 yd. background). Add borders to this to make larger quilts.

CREATIVE OPTION:
A border may be added to any of these quilts above and it will increase the dimensions by 15″ in each direction - making a quilt one size larger.

For the first border cut 3″ wide strips. The middle border is comprised of 3″ cut scrap squares used in the quilt itself. The outer border is the same as the first border.

Around the Twist

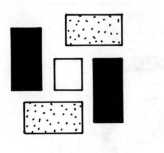

1.

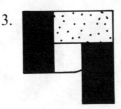

2.

3.

4.

5.

This quilt is very similar to the Snowball quilt. Instead of alternating the Snowball blocks with a Nine Patch, the Twist block has been substituted. This block appears to be difficult to piece, yet it is very easy.

There are four rectangles and one square in this Twist block.

1. To piece it, take any of the rectangles and sew it to the square, only halfway down the square.

2. Open it up and sew the second strip from edge to edge.

3 and 4. Keep adding the remaining rectangles making sure to begin and end matched.

5. Go back and close up the unfinished seam.

The three-color Around the Twist is the easiest to piece. All the Twist blocks are pieced the same, and two different Snowball blocks are used. If this quilt is set diagonally, every other row has different fabrics in the Snowball blocks. The Twist blocks are just turned in different directions as the rows are assembled.

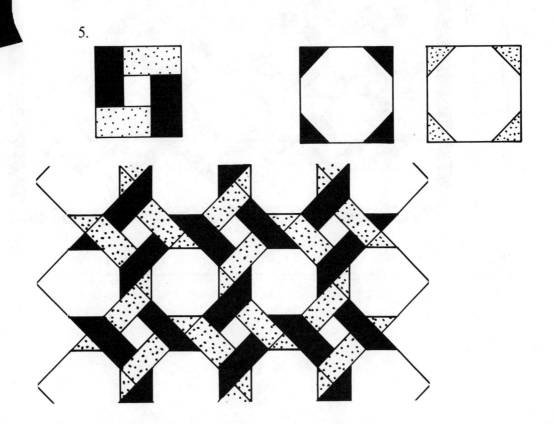

77

Large Quilt — Piecing finishes 73½″ by 94½″.
With borders it finishes 94″ by 115″.

Fabrics Required

Background — 6½ yds. (5 yds. for piecing, 1½ yds. for borders)

Main Fabric — 4 yds. (2 yds. for piecing, 2 yds. for borders and binding)

Accent Fabric — 12½ yds. (2 yds. for piecing, 10½ yds. for backing and last border)

Cutting Requirements

Background

1. Cut 13 strips 8" wide into 63 squares 8". Using the 2½" SPEEDY, cut 3 corners off 24 squares, cut 4 corners off 35 squares, and cut 2 corners off 4 squares for the corners.

2. Cut 3 strips 12" wide into 7 squares 12". Cut these squares with an X yielding 28 setting triangles. This will not float the design.

3. Cut 2 squares 8½" diagonally to yield 4 corners.

4. Cut 4 strips 3" wide into 48 squares 3" for the Twist blocks.

5. Cut 10 strips 4" wide for the 2nd border.

Main

1. Cut 14 strips 3" wide into 96 rectangles 3" by 5½" for the Twist blocks.

2. Cut 5 strips 3⅜" wide into 55 squares. Then cut these squares diagonally to yield 110 triangles for the Snowball blocks.

3. Cut 9 strips 3" wide for 1st border.

4. Cut 11 strips 2½" wide for binding.

Accent

1. Cut 14 strips 3" wide into 96 rectangles 3" by 5½" for the Twist blocks.

2. Cut 5 strips 3⅜" wide into 55 squares. Then cut these squares diagonally to yield 110 triangles for the Snowball blocks.

3. Cut 4 strips 5" wide lengthwise from the sides of the pieced back for the 3rd border.

Piecing and Assembly

1. Add the corners to the Snowball blocks. Use the diagram to see which fabrics are used in each row.

2. Assemble the Twist blocks.

3. Assemble into rows, sew rows together.

4. Add borders.

Crib Quilt — Piecing finishes to 34″ by 42″. With borders it finishes to 39″ by 47½″.

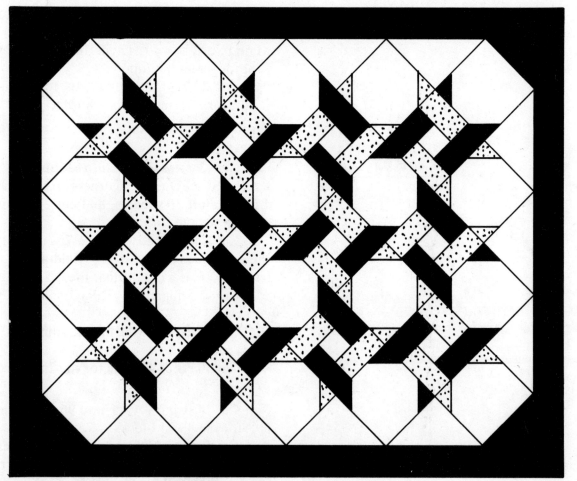

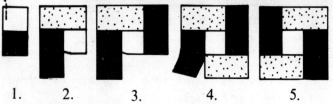

1.   2.   3.   4.   5.

Fabrics Required

Background — 1½ yds.

Main — 1¼ yds. (¾ yd. for piecing, ½ yd. for border)

Accent — 1 yd. (½ yd. for piecing, ½ yd. for binding)

Backing — 1½ yds.

Cutting Requirements

Background

1. Cut 4 strips 6½″ wide into 20 squares 6½″. Use the 2″ SPEEDY to cut 4 corners off 6 squares, 3 corners off of 10 squares, and 2 corners off 4 squares.

2. Cut 1 strip 2½″ wide into 12 squares 2½″.

3. Cut 1 strip 9¾″ wide into 4 squares 9¾″. Cut these squares with an X to yield 14 setting triangles.

Main

1. Cut 3 strips 2½″ wide into 24 rectangles 2½″ by 4½″ for Twist blocks.

2. Cut 2 strips 2⅞″ wide into 16 squares 2⅞″. Cut these squares diagonally into 31 Snowball triangles blocks.

3. Cut 2 squares 7″ once diagonally for the 4 corners.

4. Cut 5 strips 3″ wide for borders.

Accent

1. Cut 3 strips 2½″ wide into 24 rectangles 2½″ by 4½″ for Twist blocks.

2. Cut 2 strips 2⅞″ wide into 16 squares 2⅞″. Cut these into 31 triangles for Snowball blocks.

3. Cut 5 strips 2½″ wide for binding.

Piecing and Assembly

1. Add the triangles to the 20 Snowball blocks.

2. Piece the 12 Twist blocks.

3. Piece into rows, join rows.

4. Add corners last.

5. Add borders.

Lap Quilt — Piecing finishes 42½″ by 59½″. With borders, quilt finishes 49″ by 66″.

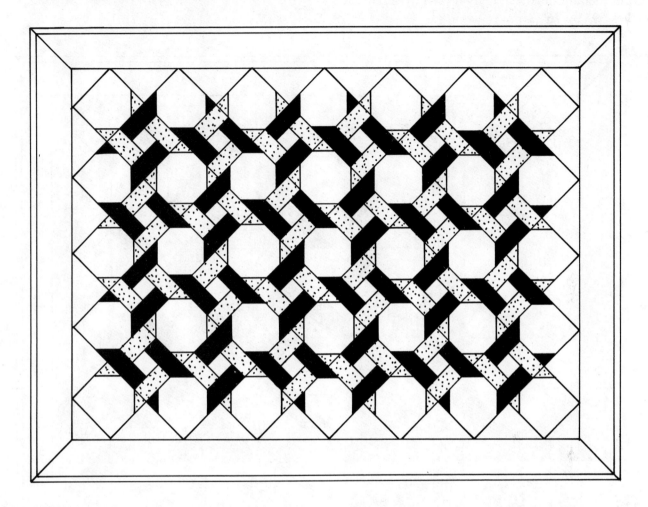

Fabrics Required

Background — 2¼ yds.
Main - 5 yds. (1 yd. for piecing, 4 yds. for back and border)
Accent — 1¾ yds. (1 yd. for piecing, ¾ yd. for binding)

Cutting Requirements

Background

1. Cut 6 strips 6½″ wide into 35 squares 6½″. Using a 2″ SPEEDY, cut 4 corners off 15 squares, cut 3 corners off 16, and cut 2 corners off 4 squares.

2. Cut 2 strips 2½″ wide. Cut these into 24 squares 2½″ for center of Twist blocks.

3. Cut 2 strips 10″ wide into 5 squares 10″. Cut these with an X to yield 20 setting triangles. This will float the design.

4. Cut 2 squares 7″ diagonally to yield the 4 corners.

Main

1. Cut 6 strips 2½″ wide into 48 rectangles 2½″ by 4½″.

2. Cut 3 strips 2⅞″ wide into 29 squares 2⅞″. Cut these squares diagonally to yield 58 triangles for the Snowball blocks.

3. Cut 4 strips 3½″ wide lengthwise from the sides of the pieced back for the borders.

Accent

1. Cut 6 strips 2½″ wide into 48 rectangles 2½″ by 4½″.

2. Cut 3 strips 2⅞″ wide into 29 squares 2⅞″. Cut these squares diagonally to yield 58 triangles for the Snowball blocks.

3. Cut 7 strips 2½″ wide for the binding.

Piecing and Assembly

1. Sew the 24 Twist blocks and the 35 Snowball blocks.

2. Piece into rows, join rows, add corners.

81

For a Real Challenge, Try a Five-Color Version

Quilt piecing finishes 51″ by 68″. With border it finishes 59″ by 76″.

The trick here is to notice that there are two different Twist blocks. Although they both use the same fabrics, they are not sewn in the same order.

Be sure to follow the diagram to ensure that these blocks will twist properly. Notice also that the setting triangles have been pieced as well. Use the same SPEEDY as for the Snowball blocks.

Fabrics Required

Background (black) — 3¼ yds. (2½ yds. for piecing, ¾ yd. for binding)
Fabric A (gold), B (green), and D (blue) — ¾ yds.
Fabric C (red) — 1¾ yds. (¾ yd. for piecing, 1 yd. for borders)
Backing — 3¾ yds. (pieced crosswise)

Cutting Requirements

Background

1. Cut 6 strips 6½″ wide into 35 squares 6½″. Use the 2″ SPEEDY to cut the corners off. Cut 4 corners off all squares.

2. Cut 3 strips 2½″ wide into 48 squares 2½″ for Twist blocks.

3. Cut 2 strips 11″ wide into 6 squares 11″. Cut these with an X to yield 24 setting triangles. Using the 2″ SPEEDY, cut the corners off these. The design will float.

4. Cut 2 squares 7″ with 1 diagonal for corners.

5. Cut 8 strips 2½″ wide for binding.

Fabric A

1. Cut 6 strips 2½″ wide into 48 rectangles 2½″ by 4½″ for Twist blocks.

2. Cut 2 strips 2⅞″ wide into 21 squares 2⅞″ and cut these diagonally into 42 triangles.

Fabric B

1. Cut 6 strips 2½″ wide into 48 rectangles 2½″ by 4½″ for the Twist blocks.

2. Cut 2 strips 2⅞″ wide into 20 squares 2⅞″. Cut these diagonally to yield 40 triangles.

Fabric C

1. Cut 6 strips 2½″ wide into 48 rectangles 2½″ by 4½″ for Twist blocks.

2. Cut 2 strips 2⅞″ wide into 17 squares 2⅞″. Cut these diagonally to yield 34 triangles.

3. Cut 7 strips 4½″ wide for borders.

Fabric D

1. Cut 6 strips 2½″ wide into 48 rectangles 2½″ by 4½″ for Twist blocks.

2. Cut 2 strips 2⅞″ wide into 24 squares 2⅞″. Cut these diagonally to yield 48 triangles.

Piecing and Assembly

1. Piece 24 of the Twist blocks to look like this:

2. Piece the other 24 Twist blocks to look like this:

3. Piece 18 Snowball blocks to look like this, with the opposite corners of fabrics A and B.

4. Piece 17 Snowball blocks to look like this, with opposite corners of fabrics C and D.

5. Add small triangles of fabric A to 6 setting triangles.

6. Add small triangles of fabric B to 4 setting triangles.

7. Add small triangles of fabric D to 14 setting triangles.

8. Piece blocks into rows according to the diagram, being careful to use the right twists on the right rows. Join the rows.

9. Add corners and borders.

Judy's Star

Large Quilt — Piecing finishes 51″ by 64″. With borders it will finish approximately 75″ by 96″.

Fabrics Required

Background — 6¾ yds. (3¾ yds. for piecing, and 3 yds. for borders)

Dark - 2¾ yds. (¾ yd. for piecing, 2 yds. for borders and binding)

Medium — 1½ yds. (¾ yd. for piecing, ¾ yd. for borders)

Backing — 6 yds.

Cutting Requirements

Background

1. Cut off 3 yds. for 3rd border and cut lengthwise into 4 strips 6½″ wide.

2. Cut 3 strips 9½″ wide into 11 squares 9½″.

3. Cut 2 strips 14″ wide into 5 squares 14″ and cut with an X. You will need 18 setting triangles. These will not float.

4. Cut 11 strips 3½″ wide into 125 squares 3½″.

5. Cut a 24″ square to be used for quarter-square triangles. Set aside.

6. Cut 1 strip 9½″ wide for extensions for the pillow area.

Dark

1. Cut 5 strips 3⅞″ wide into 50 squares 3⅞″. Then cut diagonally into 100 triangles.

2. Cut 8 strips 4½″ wide for 2nd border.

3. Cut 10 strips 2½″ wide for 1st border.

Medium

1. Cut a 24″ square to be used with same size background to make quarter-square triangles.

2. Cut 7 strips 2½″ wide for binding.

Piecing and Assembly

1. Put the 24″ squares of the background and medium fabrics right sides together and draw 25 squares 4¼″. Draw an X through all the squares and sew for quarter-square triangles. You will need 100 pairs.

2. Refer to diagram and piece 25 blocks (5 will be used for the pillow area).

3. Sew blocks together with setting triangles into rows, and join rows.

4. Add the first 2 borders.

5. Add extra 9½″ wide background fabric to the row of 5 blocks. Sew to top of quilt and cut to correct length.

6. Add 3rd border all around.

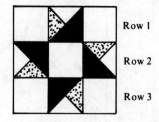

Row 1

Row 2

Row 3

Wall Hanging — Piecing finishes to 25½″ by 38¼″.
Borders build it out to approximately 41″ by 54″.

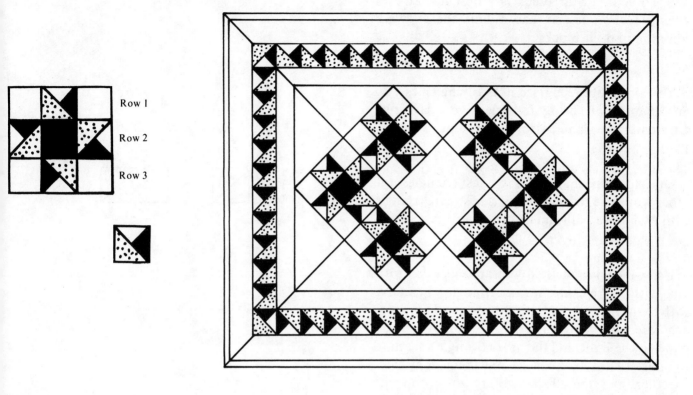

Fabrics Required

Background — 1¾ yds.

Dark — 1½ yds. (¾ yd. for piecing, ¾ yd. for borders)

Medium — 1 yd. (½ yd. for piecing, ½ yd. for binding)

Backing — 1¾ yds.

Cutting Requirements

Background

1. Cut 1 square 9½″.

2. Cut 1 strip 14″ wide into 3 squares 14″. Cut these squares with an X. You will need 10 setting triangles. These will not float.

3. Cut 2 strips 3½″ wide into 24 squares 3½″.

4. Cut a ½ yd. piece and set aside for quarter-square triangles.

Dark

1. Cut a ½ yd. piece and set aside to be sewn with background for quarter-square triangles.

2. Cut 1 strip 3½″ wide into 6 squares 3½″.

3. Cut 1st borders (2¾″ wide strips for sides, and 2⅜″ strips for the top and bottom). This difference will help the pieced border be mathematically compatible with the pieced area of the top. The second set of dark borders is all cut 2½″ wide to be put on after the pieced border.

Medium

1. Cut 4 strips 3⅞″ wide into 38 squares 3⅞″. Then cut these diagonally to yield 76 triangles.

2. Cut 6 strips 2½″ wide for binding.

Piecing and Assembly

1. Put the two ½-yd. pieces of the dark and background right sides together and draw 19 squares 4¼″. Draw an X through the squares and sew for quarter-square triangles. You will need 76 pairs.

2. Refer to diagram and piece 6 complete blocks and 52 border units.

3. Sew blocks together with setting triangles into rows, and join rows.

4. Add 1st dark border, then the pieced border, and then the last dark border.

87

Evening Star with Snowball

The Evening Star block is a design that uses several techniques. It has a unit that is very common in quilt blocks.

You probably recognize it as Flying Geese. In the chapter on using triangles, you saw two different methods to assemble this unit.

One would be made with two fast triangles, the other would be to use one quarter-square triangle with two loose half-square triangles.

Use whichever method you are most comfortable with. I like using two fast triangles. I can live with the seam down the middle because I am more accurate with the triangles. I iron one triangle's seam to the light and the other triangle's seam to the dark. That way when I put them right sides together my seam allowances are going opposite directions, and I always have a ¼" seam allowance for the top peak.

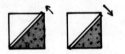

The block is easily pieced together in rows:

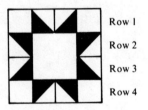

Row 1
Row 2
Row 3
Row 4

By itself, it does not make great-looking quilts. When mixed with a version of the Snowball block, the quilt takes on a very different look. Most people will have trouble picking out the quilt layout.

Large Quilt — Piecing finishes to 56″ by 88″. With borders it finishes to 72″ by 104″.

Fabrics Required

Background — 4¼ yds.

Dark — 5¼ yds. (1¾ yds. for piecing, 3½ yds for borders)

Accent — 1¾ yds. (¾ yd. for piecing, 1 yd. for binding)

Backing — 6¼ yds.

Cutting Requirements

Background

1. Cut 10 strips 8½″ wide into 39 squares 8½″. Using the 2″ SPEEDY, cut all 4 corners off each square.

2. Cut 10 strips 2½″ wide into 152 squares 2½″.

3. Cut a 1-yd. piece and set aside for the fast triangles.

Dark

1. Cut off 3½ yds. for the border and cut that piece lengthwise into 4 strips 8½″ wide.

2. Cut 6 strips 2⅞″ wide, then cut into 78 squares 2⅞″. Cut these squares diagonally to get the 156 loose triangles (for the Snowball corners).

3. Cut a 1-yd. piece and set aside for the fast triangles.

Accent

1. Cut 5 strips 4½″ wide into 38 squares 4½″.

2. Cut 10 strips 3½″ wide for binding.

Piecing and Assembly

1. Put the 1-yd. pieces of dark and background fabric right sides together and mark a grid 12 X 13 of 2⅞″ squares. Sew, cut apart, and iron. You will need 304 triangle units.

NOTE: If you find this piece too large to handle easily, you could break it up into smaller parts before you sew.

2. Piece 39 Snowball blocks and 38 Star blocks.

3. Assemble rows according to diagram.

4. Add borders.

Wall hanging — Piecing finishes to 30″ by 30″.
With borders it finishes to 40″ by 40″.

Fabrics Required

Background — 1 yd.
Dark — ½ yd.
Medium — 1¼ yds. (½ yd. for piecing, ¾ yd. for border and binding)
Stripe — 4 lengths 1½ yds. long
Back — 1¼ yds.

Cutting Requirements

Background
1. Cut 2 strips 6½″ wide into 12 squares 6½″. Cut 4 corners off each square using the 1½″ SPEEDY.
2. Cut 3 strips 2″ wide into 52 squares 2″.
3. Set aside remainder of piece for fast triangles.

Dark
1. Cut 2 strips 3½″ wide into 13 squares 3½″.
2. Cut 2 strips 2⅜″ wide into 24 squares 2⅜″. Cut these squares diagonally to get 48 loose triangles.

Medium
1. Cut 4 strips 1½″ wide for 1st border.
2. Cut 4 strips 2½″ wide for binding.
3. Set aside ½ yd. for fast triangles.

Stripe — You will need 4 lengths of stripe (1½ yds. each).

Piecing and Assembly

1. Put the fast triangle pieces of background and medium fabric together, and mark a grid 6 squares by 9 squares 2⅜″. Sew, cut apart, and iron. You will need 104 triangle units.
2. Piece 13 Star blocks and 12 Snowball blocks.
3. Assemble rows according to diagram.
4. Add borders.

Devil's Claw

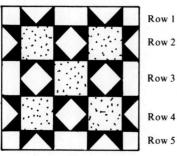

Row 1
Row 2
Row 3
Row 4
Row 5

Quilt Size — Piecing finishes 51″ by 68″. With borders it finishes approximately 72″ by 102″.

This quilt block is really made up of four Evening Star blocks. The triangles are small, so you want to be careful in handling them. The block is pieced in rows.

This quilt uses twelve of these blocks set diagonally with five larger Evening Star blocks falling across the pillow area.

Fabrics Requirements

Background — 7 yds. (4½ yds. for piecing and 2½ yds. for borders and binding)

Main (star points) — 1½ yd. (1¼ yd. for piecing, ¼ yd. for border around pillow area)

Accent — 2½ yds. (1 yd. for piecing, 1½ yds. for borders)

Backing — 6¼ yds.

Cutting Requirements

Background

1. Cut 3 strips 2″ wide into 48 squares 2″.

2. Cut 2 strips 3″ wide into 20 squares 3″ for pillow area.

3. Cut 4 strips 2″ wide into 48 rectangles 2″ by 3½″.

4. Cut 6 strips 4¼″ wide into 48 squares 4¼″. Cut these with an X to yield the 192 quarter-square triangles.

5. Cut 1 strip 6¼″ wide into 5 squares 6¼″. Cut these with an X to yield 20 quarter-square triangles to use in the pillow area.

6. Cut 2 strips 12½″ wide into 6 squares 12½″.

7. Cut 2 strips 18¼″ wide into 3 squares 18¼″. Cut these with an X to yield 10 setting triangles. This will not float.

8. Cut 2 squares 13″ once diagonally for corners.

9. Cut 1 strip 10½″ wide for extensions for pillow area.

10. Cut 10 strips 6½″ wide for 2nd border if cutting cross-grain. (You might want to cut them lengthwise and set aside first.)

11. Cut 10 strips 2½″ wide for binding.

Main

1. Cut 12 strips 2⅜″ wide into 192 squares 2⅜″. Cut the squares diagonally to yield 384 triangles.

2. Cut 2 strips 3⅜″ wide into 20 squares 3⅜″. Cut these diagonally to yield 40 triangles for pillow area.

3. Cut 3 strips 2″ wide for border in pillow area.

Accent

1. Cut 6 strips 3½″ wide into 60 squares 3½″.

2. Cut 1 strip 5½″ wide into 5 squares 5½″ for pillow area.

3. Cut 9 strips 5″ wide for 1st border.

Piecing and Assembly

1. Sew the small half-square triangles to the quarter-square triangles. Join these units with the other cut squares and piece the blocks in rows.

2. Join blocks with plain blocks and setting triangles to form rows. Join rows.

3. Add 1st border.

4. Piece 5 Evening Star blocks for pillow area. Join these into 1 strip. Add border all around. Add on extensions of background to each side of strip. Measure and cut off to match quilt with its 1st border.

5. Add 2nd border all around.

1.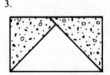

2.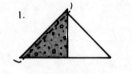
Hit intersection right here

3.

BIOGRAPHY

Trudie J. Hughes

The author, Trudie Hughes, is interested in adapting modern techniques to the beautiful craft of quiltmaking. She feels strongly that time-saving techniques allow the modern woman to more easily finish large quilting projects. She became interested in quilting when she was in high school, when her father, a mathematics teacher, stimulated her interest in geometry. Trudie was intrigued by the mathematics of quiltmaking. She received a B.A. degree in home economics, where her major interest was textiles. After college, she moved to Wisconsin, and became more and more active in quiltmaking activities. Trudie currently owns a quilt shop, Patched Works, Inc., which she started in 1977. She is active in teaching, writing, and quilting. She lives in Elm Grove, Wisconsin, with her husband Jack and their two teen-age sons.

The ROTARY RULE™ is available through Patched Works, 13330 Watertown Plank Rd., Elm Grove, Wisconsin 53122.

That Patchwork Place Publications

Barnyard Beauties by Mary Ann Farmer
Basics of Quilted Clothing by Nancy Martin
Bearwear by Nancy J. Martin
Branching Out - Tree Quilts by Carolann Palmer (April 1986)
Cathedral Window - A New View by Mary Ryder Kline
Christmas Classics by Sue Saltkill
Christmas Quilts by Marsha McCloskey
Country Christmas by Sue Saltkill
Fabriscapes™ by Gail Johnson
Feathered Star Sampler by Marsha McCloskey
Housing Projects by Nancy J. Martin
Linens and Old Lace by Nancy Martin and Sue Saltkill
Make a Medallion by Kathy Cook
Pieces of the Past by Nancy J. Martin (June 1986)
Pilots, Partners & Pals by Mary Ann Farmer
Projects for Blocks and Borders by Marsha McCloskey
Quilter's Christmas by Nancyann Twelker
Sew Special by Susan A. Grosskopf
Small Quilts by Marsha McCloskey
Special Santas by Mary Ann Farmer
Stencil Patch by Nancy Martin
Touch of Fragrance by Marine Bumbalough
Wall Quilts by Marsha McCloskey
Warmest Witches to You by Mary Ann Farmer

For more information, send $2 for our color catalog to That Patchwork Place, Inc., P.O. Box 118, Bothell, WA 98041-0118, or check with your local quilt shop.

Printed in the United States of America